A Night of Massacre

A Night of Massacre

Copyright © 2024 by A R Sarkar

ISBN: 9798339956075

Website: www.arsarkar.com

Book Cover by Deepesh Sarkar

Book Design by Deepesh Sarkar

First edition: 2024

I dedicate this novel to the feet of my mentor, my inspiration, my late father Sudhir Chandra Sarkar.

PROLOGUE

This is in a Hindi-speaking state of Eastern India - where untouchability, casteism, and many superstitions still prevail in contemporary society - where peace has been disrupted by the force of truncheons and guns, justice overshadowed by injustice - where today, the political macabre for winning elections is accompanied by intense oppression and suffering - where the right to protest seems to belong only to those who either run their own organizations or are directly or indirectly associated with those organizations where the proverb 'might is right' truly holds sway - where an impartial life is proclaimed impossible.

In such a backdrop, is my protagonist Damodar Poddar aka Damu - a *Dalit* youth whose language of protest is mute, whose mind is affected by internal conflict about emancipation from inferiority and the desire for self-empowerment.

What did he want to do? And what game did destiny play with him? In Damu's life, a single day's occurrences form the basis of my story where there is only the unfolding of incidents - no remedy for upcoming evils.

- A. R. Sarkar

A Night of Massacre

Just like yesterday, Damu was wandering the streets early in the morning. Extreme internal conflict, sorrow, inferiority complex, and anger had robbed him of his sleep. His head felt like it was going to explode. It was summer. Across the vast fields, the sun peeked out past the brick kiln chimney left behind the trees. This happened every day, but today it seemed to Damu that the chimney might not let the sun rise. To him, the kiln owner and the chimney seemed the same— selfish, exploitative, tyrannical and many other things that didn't appear in his vocabulary at this point, perhaps because he had fallen into the vortex of time twelve years before and never made it past seventh grade in his school. This realization felt like salt on an open wound. He kicked a half-brick lying in the middle of the dirt road with his worn-out flip-flop. The pain didn't register with his restless nerves, but as he looked up, he realized he had reached the banyan tree near the abandoned swampy pond outside the village of the hundred-odd houses.

As he stared at the tree for a moment, the pain in his foot seemed to shift to a dull ache in his chest. It was all because of yesterday. Puja's tear-filled, pleading eyes appeared before him; her face, wet with tears running down her cheeks. Only then he began to recall the entire incident.

***

Puja, with her flowing locks, had pulled Damu close. "If you come a little closer, will your caste..." She realized her mistake before finishing the sentence and, looking at Damu's dry, indifferent face, snapped her fingers, saying, "Hey!"

Damu, pulled from his melancholy reflection, replied, "I feel scared – rather, your caste will be compromised. Will people let us live together? I am *Dalit* and –"

Puja's fair, soft hand pressed against Damu's dark face. The beautiful Brahmin girl stopped him mid-sentence.

"Swear on my life that you will never say it again. I love you – I want to have you – let the blame be mine – I don't care about anything else."

A small flicker of happiness, gathered deep within the heart, had appeared as a faint smile on Damu's face. Like many a time, just as Puja felt the desire to surrender herself by resting her head on Damu's chest smiling a longing smile, someone whistled like the so-called riffraff in the front row of a cinema hall, causing them to separate from each other.

Just as a woman's dormant emotions are intense, so are her open conflicts. Therefore, Puja was the first to stand up. As Damu got to his feet, he saw Bilton Singh emerge from behind one of the trees that had grown tall around the pond, which lay abandoned due to a dispute over acquiring the government land between two wealthy men. Two of his constant henchmen appeared from behind the other trees—one a thug by nature, and the other a mix of thug and joker.

Bilton's sharp rebuke rang out in anger at the spontaneous whistling, "Damn it, you ruined such a good Sunday show! What a fool you are!"

Even though Puja had composed herself, her face betrayed the clear signs of impending danger. Despite being preoccupied with worries about Puja, Damu felt a surge of irritation at the sight of Bilton. It seemed to him there might be a confrontation today. But a sense of guilt left him feeling somewhat helpless. Seizing the opportunity, Bilton, dropping his usual thug persona, attempted to be a bit humorous, throwing out a sarcastic remark, "Hey there,

Keshtomaharaj, are you playing around with her for fun? Forcing yourself, perhaps? Just look at the girl's face—how pale she's gone! Poor thing!" After his comment ended, a sly smile appeared on his face, as if with some cunning plan. He told his goon, "Give him a slap, a loud one. That'll knock some sense into him. We've caught *Keshtomaharaj* red-handed today. What are you waiting for? Hit him!"

The mixed-character thug, signalling his accomplice to follow the boss's orders, gestured for the other thug to raise his hand to deliver a slap. As the other thug moved to strike, Damu grabbed his hand. Although Damu had the strength to take on two such men, he was merely attempting to defend himself at that moment. Bilton stepped forward and pushed Damu back to diminish his defiance. The two henchmen watched with growing enthusiasm. Seeing their eagerness, Bilton shoved Damu again and sneered, "Hey! Showing some arrogance, huh?"

Damu's jaw tightened, and his eyes seemed to blaze with anger. It seemed he was on the brink of losing control. But then, Bilton's taunting words took on a threatening tone, "Hey, showing me those eyes? Worrying so much about yourself!

Have you ever thought about your home? Those five houses your mother works in, you know —"

At the mention of his mother, all of Damu's anger turned into astonishment. As he looked questioningly at Bilton, Bilton continued, completing his half-spoken sentence, "—if I get her fired from those houses, what will happen to your crippled father? Have you ever thought about that? Even with what you and your sister earn together, you can barely afford your *dal* and *roti*. On top of that, where will your father's medicines come from?"

The two henchmen nodded in agreement with their boss's arrogant speech, expressing their satisfaction. Puja, besides being a sorrowful mute spectator, had no other choice at this moment. Damu's inner self now forced him to bow his head. Bilton continued relentlessly, "A dwarf shouldn't try to reach the moon. You fool, don't you know that? 'Dalit'—you are a 'Dalit'— you understand that? Come on, come on, get lost. Such happiness isn't meant for people like you. Move along."

Damu's eyes welled up. Looking through his blurry vision at Puja, he saw tears streaming down her cheeks, but she remained silent. The faint hope of direct sympathy dissolved deep within him. Helplessly and with a pained heart, Damu moved away as the mixed-character henchman mockingly gestured for him to get lost. The sounds of Bilton and the other two's loud laughter followed him, echoing in his ears.

***

Even more than the empty space under the tree, Damu felt an emptiness in his chest. A crow cawed and suddenly flew away. With teary eyes, Damu murmured to himself a philosophical reflection of Bilton's words from the previous day, "Is such happiness meant for us?" He then continued to walk on, lost in thought. But for a moment, he wondered if leaving Puja had been the right thing to do. In the next instant, he reassured himself, thinking about what else he could have done.

***

Puja, having just finished her morning bath, was hanging wet clothes to dry on the line in the courtyard. Her towel was wrapped around her head in a way that made her look like a film model fresh out of the bath. The sun seemed to add a radiant glow to her face, highlighting her features like a quintessential Brahmin girl. As she shook her long, loose hair and let it fall over her chest, preparing to hang the towel to dry, she suddenly felt a sharp pang in her chest—her face went pale. Through the gap between her towel and *kurta*, she thought she saw someone known!

Yes, Damu was walking towards her with hesitant steps. This was the path he often took. Through the gaps in the thorny fence, passersby were easily recognizable. Damu paused for a moment, his eyes seeming to blur again. The dull ache in his chest perhaps echoed once more, "Is such happiness even meant for us...?" With that, Damu's feet resumed their slow, reluctant pace.

Tears welled up in Puja's eyes, filled with shame and sorrow for not being able to stand by Damu's side yesterday. But what could she have done? That scoundrel Bilton would have humiliated him even more, perhaps turning his threats into reality. And what would have become of Damu then? But, ugh! That vile creature—Puja recalled every corrupt step of Bilton Singh, filled with filth and degradation.

Puja's mind filled with the memory of each vile action of Bilton Singh.

***

As Puja's tear-filled eyes blurred the image of Damu walking away, the loud laughter of the three scoundrels pierced her ears, feeding the monster of fear rising from the depths of her heart. Her legs felt stiff and heavy. Bilton's henchmen, still laughing, followed his signal and moved in the opposite direction of Damu's path. Yet, Bilton's mocking words were not done.

"And you, oh dear! Shedding tears for the love of that insignificant, uneducated brute? 'Strange'!"

Accustomed to using a few commonly known English words like 'strange,' though not completely fluent, Bilton often interspersed his speech with them, thanks to his direct connection with the big city.

Puja tried to muster courage and steady herself, but as soon as she looked up, Bilton's deliberate taunting continued. "—Do you know what will happen if this gets out in the village? Hey, today—" Pulling out his mobile phone from one of the loose pockets of his multi-pocket baggy jeans, he continued gesturing with his hand, "—there are these mobile phones, computers are running. But a village is still a village. Everyone will spit on you. And then, forget about getting married; you'll have to leave the village with your - wife-less,

- drunkard father. Yes, 'that is right.'" Though he hesitated briefly, his satisfaction with using the simple version equivalent for 'widowed' as it added corroboration to his previous remarks, made his mannerism phrase 'that is right' come out spontaneously. Puja's courage seemed to vanish once more.

"But no," Puja's lost courage seemed to transfer into Bilton, doubling in strength. "I won't let that happen." A cunning smile spread across his face. "I will save you—" He stepped closer, stopping right in front of Puja and repeated, "I will save you. Day and night, I think about you. Let me have a bit of that in return."

Startled by the sudden shift in Bilton's tone from mocking to emotional, Puja frowned in confusion.

Bilton's eyes were filled with lust, and he lost the distinction between formal and informal address. "I want to have you—"

As Puja moved to escape, Bilton, in a futile attempt to alter his emotional tone, finished his sentence, "—Yes, like a friend. Just hug me once—like a friend—." His eyes burned with desire, and with a trembling tongue and quivering lips, he stammered while looking around nervously and, suddenly and unexpectedly, grabbing Puja, mumbled, "That's all I want—just once—"

Puja, mustering all her strength to free herself, kept shouting, "Let go, let me go, I'm telling you,"But Bilton didn't hear a word. Even the distant ringing of a bicycle bell didn't register with him. He tightened his grip with trembling hands, rubbing them against Puja's back, and quickly unzipped the top of her *kameez* with a sudden jerk. In a desperate, tangled voice, he moaned, "Just once—only once—nothing more."

Before the words were fully out of his mouth, Puja summoned all her strength and let out a fierce, womanly roar, managing to free herself. Holding the open zipper on her fair bare back, she sprinted towards the road. Just then, the bicycle bell rang again, and a string of curses erupted from Bilton's throat like the hiss and sizzle of a fire suddenly quenched by water, "You tease, showing off your airs – how long do you think—"

Noticing the cyclist, Bilton quickly hid behind a tree, cutting off his incomplete remark. Pulling up the open zipper on her *kameez*, Puja turned around and stumbled right in front of the bicycle. Trying to steady himself while glancing at embarrassed Puja, the cyclist, lost his balance and crashed to the ground with his bike.

***

As Puja watched Damu moving farther away from her house with blurry eyes, she remembered that she had only heard the sound of the cyclist falling because she had then been forced to flee, thinking 'every man for himself'.

***

Though the sun was out, the little light filtering through the small, window-like openings couldn't fully dispel the darkness inside Damu's house. The stark contrast between the open, spacious flats catering to increased urban demands in a city and these numerous poor houses in the village was a vivid example of the 'sky-earth difference.' Here, the need for a beautiful abode was a far-fetched dream for people focused only on survival.

Some random old clothes hung from a bamboo inserted between two walls. Various everyday items lay scattered around. A full-length pant and a long-sleeve shirt, probably Damu's only outdoor attire, hung from a nail driven into the mud wall. One section of the inner part housed a kerosene stove and some cheap utensils, indicating a kitchen, while the other section had a cot with a couple of saris—one white and one coloured—marking the shared sleeping space of Damu's mother, Raimoni, and his elder sister, Sandhya. The front part, with a wooden cot covered with quilts, was clearly the designated spot for Damu's father, Hariram Poddar, implying that Damu had to sleep on the floor. Under these circumstances, in one corner, under the old dhoti and shirt hanging from the bamboo pole, a small, half-broken stool held a small idol of Lord Krishna. Its serene smile seemed to symbolize the acceptance of unavoidable fate and the will of the divine, echoing the often-recited but seldom understood verse from the Hindu scripture, the Gita: "*Karmanyevadhikaraste Ma Phaleshu Kadachana*" ("You have the right to perform your actions, but never to the fruits or outcomes thereof.").

From outside, the sound of Hariram's coughing could be heard. After bathing her husband with water she had stored, Raimoni brought him inside bearing almost the entire weight of his body on her shoulders and placed him on the cot, saying, "Take it easy."

Hariram, with his entire right side paralyzed, released the stick made from a tree branch that he had been holding with his left hand and lay down, replying, "Alright then."

Raimoni appeared to be a woman of a rather fiery temperament, and perhaps that was not surprising. When a woman bears the full weight of household responsibilities amidst extreme poverty, her body and soul gradually become as dry and hardened as a coconut left to desiccate. Just as a green coconut, once full of nourishing water and tender pulp, eventually transforms into a tough and brittle shell when dried, so too has Raimoni become—weathered and rigid under the relentless strain. Only God knows what lies beneath the surface. Abruptly, she interrupted and, with a stern expression, said, "Alright— yes, it's exactly as it should be. You've taken on every malady the world has to offer."

Hariram, long accustomed to such exchanges, fumbled with his left hand under the bed, searching for the half-empty bundle of *bidis* and the old lighter that Damu had brought. Defending himself, he muttered, "Hey, does a person invite sickness from God by choice?"

As Raimoni went to cover his legs with a sheet, her eyes fell on the bidi. That was it. Dropping the sheet, she snatched the bundle of *bidis* and snapped, "No, not by choice, you forcibly snatch it. How many times has the doctor told you to quit these things? You have asthma – heart problems. Smoking increases your cough. Increased cough raises blood pressure, and blood pressure – oh, who can explain it to you! It's useless – oh God!"

Whenever Hariram's mental balance was disturbed, his coughing would start up immediately. As he coughed and coughed, he weakly protested, "Alright, alright, stop now. Once you start, you never—"

Raimoni cut him off, "Never stop, right? Of course! The burden is all on my shoulders. What do you have to worry about? Our widowed daughter goes to work and—"

As she turned her head, she saw Damu at the door, and her anger flared up even more. She glared at Damu. "Look at this, oh God! What's this? Have you become a lord now? Do you think food will appear just by sitting at home?"

Hariram's support always lay with his only son, Damu. "Let him at least come inside," he said and then called out himself, "Come in."

For some unknown reason, who knows why, Raimoni's anger seemed unusually intense today. She scolded her husband sharply, "Be quiet. You were the one who spoiled him by your support and put him in this position." Then, turning her barrage of questions back at Damu, she asked, "Yes, tell me, will food appear by doing like this?"

Has Damu who is over twenty-four, also lost his calm today? He shot back with a sharp retort, "So, if I go to work, will I get gold and jewels?"

Raimoni chewed over the sarcasm and spat back, "No, you won't get gold and jewels. But at least you can hope for a dry piece of bread."

"Dry bread! Huh—after starving to death? They're not even paying wages. Work hard and starve harder."

"Sandhya is still going, isn't she?"

"She doesn't have much in her head. Being that simple won't work. If she stops going to work, the owner will be forced to take notice. But one person alone won't make a difference."

Hariram tried to suppress his cough and express

his delight. Meanwhile, it seemed as though Raimoni's natural reactions had come to a standstill. She stood, mouth slightly open, staring at Damu in an attempt to comprehend him.

Today, Damu appeared to be a rebel—a fighter. He continued, "Everyone, without any discrimination, must quit working together. Only then will the owner be forced to bow down. And if this happens everywhere, the exploitation by the employers and corrupt leaders will end. A new social system will be created. But someone, someday, has to start it. And why shouldn't that someone be me?"

After delivering his words in one breath, Damu stomped his foot and walked straight out of the house, leaving Raimoni stunned. Hariram's eyes filled with tears of joy, realizing that his son had grown up—he was now thinking beyond the confines of narrow-mindedness.

***

The black and white smoke billowing out of the towering chimney of the brick kiln seemed to reflect the sad sighs of the labourers working below. Scattered across three or four groups, men, women, and a few younger boys and girls were engrossed in their assigned tasks. A few women, balancing stacks of raw and baked bricks on their heads, moved steadily while their naked, toddling children clung to the edges of their sarees, walking alongside them in short bursts. It appeared that, save for special festivals or religious events, clothes were a rarity for these little ones. In one corner stood a small office, constructed from neatly stacked bricks. Outside, seated on a chair in front of a table, was an elderly man sporting old-fashioned pair of glasses—a figure embodying both the *Munim* (accountant) and the manager. His name was something like Tekchand, but both the owner and the workers simply knew and called him '*Munim*'.

Scattered across the table were an account ledger, a stack of forged bill books, receipt books, and a makeshift register. Not far from the table, four labourers—three old men and one man over thirty—were engaged in a low-voiced conversation. Though some of their words reached Munim's ears yet he couldn't quite grasp the full meaning, so he pretended to look elsewhere while straining to hear.

The first worker insisted, "This time, they must give us our wages. Otherwise, how will we run our households?"

The second labourer, a frail man named Banwari Lal, added to the discussion by expressing his own sorrows, "My Chaganiya (Chagan Lal) has had a fever for two days now. And today, his son, Chhuttan – my grandson – has also caught a fever. Now, an adult can tough it out without medicine, lying on the bed clenching his teeth through the illness, but children–"

The elderly Jubed Ali Khan finished the sentence, "–must be given medicine. It's been three weeks already. At least they should give us one week's wages. My shopkeeper has made it clear – no more credit. No lentils, no rice. Now we –"

The young man Ramdeen cut in with a sharp remark, "We'll just have to starve to death. No, uncle, I'm heading to the city. I'll find work in a factory. Bhanu – my brother-in-law – he's already gone. The pay is better there, and they pay on time – by the seventh of every month. They even give advances. Once I get the wages here – that's it."

Shaking his head, Banwari made his negative stance clear, "Not everyone can move to the city. We have to work here. We just need to get our wages on time."

"Uncle," Ramdeen, perhaps intentionally, waved his right hand, squinted his eyes, and raised his voice twice as loud, "Stop the work – they will be forced to give the wages. Yes."

In response to Banwari's silence and stunned gaze, the first worker and Jubed's support echoed, "Yes, that's the only way now."

Munim, who had been patiently listening, comprehended Ramdeen's words. He stood up straight and, his face always a question mark, advanced, hurling verbal jabs. "What's all this grumbling? What are you going to stop, huh? Stop work? Eh?"

Reluctantly, as if pushed into a corner, Ramdeen stammered, "And what otherwise? If we don't – get our wages – cleared up, – we will – stop working. How long – can we go on like this –"

The Munim cut him off with a sarcastic retort, "How long? As if it's been six months already? The owner is going to sell off the bricks and run away, is that it?"

"No sir, I'm not saying that. I'm just –"

"So, what exactly are you saying? Tell me."

Ramdeen stammered, "Sir, I was just saying – I mean – it's been three weeks – everyone's suffering – everyone's worried – Isn't that right, Uncle?"

The Munim's typical chewed-up, loud voice stunned everyone as he shouted, "Who's worried? Who's suffering? The wages aren't running away anywhere. Only the slackers keep harping about wages. Got it?"

Banwari defended himself, "No, Munim *ji*, that's not the case. Everyone's suffering." Then, in a slightly louder but serious tone, addressing everyone around him, he continued, "Say something now, brothers, they're labelling us as slackers."

Some labourers who were sitting and making bricks stood up to understand the situation. Those who were heading to collect bricks also stopped to listen. On Munim's questioning face, there appeared a mix of thought and surprise. Suddenly, gathering courage, the first labourer, as if seeking to take the lead, snapped, "We are not slackers. But now, we will stop working. Once we get our dues, we'll resume. What do you say, brothers?"

A murmur echoed around. From various voices, parts of the first labourer's statement blended into a chant, resonating as a slogan for "Stop the work." "Yes, yes, stop the work." "Work will resume once we get our dues." "We are not slackers."

Those carrying or fetching stacks of raw and baked bricks on their heads, fearing they might lose balance, couldn't join in the slogan but stood frozen, some casting curious glances while others stared blankly.

There was still a note of plea in Banwari's voice, "Munim-*ji*, please, at least give us some money this time."

Munim snapped, "And how exactly am I supposed to give you 'money'? Is this brick kiln my father's property?"

He opened his mouth to say more but fell silent at the loud screech of brakes from the old jeep owned by the master.

Everyone, including Munim, turned to look in that direction. The stout, heavyset, balding master stepped down from the driver's seat, walking straight toward the crowd, though his eyes scanned all around.

His name was Ratnakar Singh, which matched his mentality perfectly. As soon as the workers caught sight of the owner, they scattered in all directions, and Munim, regaining his composure, promptly shut his gaping mouth.

Damu's thirty-two-year-old childless widowed sister, Sandhya, carrying a load of raw bricks on her head, hurriedly tried to move away from Ratnakar's path but suddenly collided with a pre-adolescent twelve-year-old boy rushing from the opposite direction. The bricks lost their balance and fell to the ground, with a couple of them breaking into two pieces."

As Sandhya bent down to pick up the fallen bricks and prepare to balance them back on her head, Ratnakar's gaze fell on the bare upper part of her waist from a distance. He went straight up to the boy and gave him a shove.

"Hey! What's this? Chasing after a girl? Look at the damage you've caused! Look!" Saying this, he gave the boy another shove. The boy, only understanding the word "damage" and nothing else, lowered his head and stood there in silence.

Ratnakar's crooked gaze now landed on Sandhya's prominent bosom peeking from the folds of her white sari. Forgetting the boy, driven by a long-standing, uncontrollable desire to fondle, he suddenly reached out with his left hand and touched Sandhya's back.

"Ah-haha, did it hurt anywhere?"

In response to the situation, a woman's instinctive, lightning-fast reaction made Sandhya recoil. Initially in surprise and then with respect, she replied, "No, master."

Feeling his own failure, Ratnakar, with a bitter sense of frustration, stomped his booted feet, worn without laces, towards the main site.

Sandhya gathered the bricks and proceeded towards her destination. While most people returned to their tasks, some lingered behind, still observing with curious glances.

Ratnakar's reprimand was directed straight at Munim. "What's going on here? What are you teaching them by stopping work, Munim?"

Munim, always ready with an answer, spoke up, "Master, they are saying they will stop working." He then pointed at Ramdeen with a sarcastic remark, "And this one here is the leader."

Ratnakar also mockingly echoed the last word, "Lea-der, huh!" Then, as he scrutinized Ramdeen more closely, his demeanor completely changed. Raising his mixed brows and smiling slyly, he said, "You're Ramdeen, right? Your wife too –" Ratnakar stopped mid-sentence, intentionally. Ramdeen's limited presence of mind kicked in. "Yes, master, it's been three days now –" he stammered, "she's – not well – so she hasn't come – to work."

Ratnakar remembered a similar 'not well' day when he had a sweat-drenched incomplete copulation with Ramdeen's currently absent wife. Although incomplete, his demand at that time had been fulfilled. He had even given a full ten rupees as a tip, wiping the sweat from his face with his *dhoti*. Holding the ten-rupee-note in her fist, adjusting her sari, and pulling her veil, Ramdeen's wife had left the hot brick kiln room with a muted smile of satisfaction, having fulfilled both her physical and financial needs.

Ratnakar would often distribute such ten- or five-rupee notes to many women as payment for his incomplete or slightly complete copulations. But the case of Ramdeen's wife seemed entirely different.

To manage the mental and physical disturbances that arose from his erotic thoughts, Ratnakar regained his composure by reiterating well-known scientific facts. "Yes—yes, young women – they feel 'not well' during a certain period every month. But she does her work very well. And you, you're a good craftsman too. But what am I hearing! You've taken to reforming the society?"

In response to the entirely personal and sycophantic remark, Ramdeen lowered his head and hesitated. "Well—um—"

"Yes, yes, speak up."

Confounding everyone, Ramdeen turned his head sideways, casting a furtive glance at Banwari, and completed his sentence, "Well—uncle said— he's in great trouble —so uncle—"

With a sudden display of his true character, Ratnakar roared, "And who isn't in trouble? I am the owner of this brick kiln. I have many own troubles too. But does that mean I should shut down the kiln? And, what's with you, old man? Have you taken up the hobby of leadership in your old age? Huh?"

Banwari replied politely, "No, sir, being a leader is the work of the rich, those who know how to use both force and deceit. We are poor. We only know how to sweat it out for two meals a day."

"Shut up, scoundrel! —don't give me a speech. Just say what you want to say plainly."

"Master, we want our wages. It's been a long time. Everyone's home—"

"How long? It hasn't even been a year, right?"

Suddenly, Munim, who had been silent and nodding his head until now, chimed in, "That's what I was saying, master. I was trying to make these slackers understand."

"Enough, Munim—stop lecturing. You've explained enough. Now I'll set them straight. Listen, all of you —I will give the wages as per my will. Those who want to work, can work, and those who don't, can get lost. I will bring people from far-off villages. They will stay here and work. They will agree even if I say I will pay them after selling the goods. You ungrateful lot—I am doing you a favor by keeping you employed, and you scoundrels want to sit on my head? Shame on you!"

After delivering his heated speech, Ratnakar scanned the silent audience hoping to see the expected submissive response. Waving his hand irritably, he continued in a forceful tone, " Alright – those who don't want to work, get out now. Come back at the end of next month to settle your accounts. Ratnakar Singh has a solution for every problem. Now move—move!"

The hopeful poor workers, not wanting to lose their jobs, slowly shuffled back to their places. Needless to say, Ramdeen had already slinked away with a dry, selfish grin. Banwari and Jubed exchanged glances, silently standing together. The first worker, head bowed, walked past Ratnakar and the Munim, muttering, "Let a few more days pass. God is watching everything."

A sarcastic remark effortlessly escaped Ratnakar's lips, "Huh, God is watching, huh? If God was really watching, wouldn't He have made you a master by now?"

Satisfied that he had poured salt into the wound just right, Ratnakar laughed heartily and glanced at the two who still stood there. "What's this? Looks like you're still full of energy, aren't you?"

With a plea in his voice, Banwari said, "Master, giving us a little money won't make a difference to you. But that would at least help us get by with essentials like food."

Jubed supported him, "Yes, master, at least give us one week's wages. It was agreed that we would be paid weekly."

 Ratnakar's eyes seemed to flare up suddenly, but without revealing his thoughts, he said, "Alright — fine. Come to the office. We'll talk there." With that, he walked straight towards the office, stepping over the narrow path made of small brick fragments and ash.

Munim gave a mocking smile, motioned for the two to follow, and went off in another direction to supervise the work. Filled with hope, Banwari and Jubed made their way toward the office.

***

The office room was built with stacked baked bricks, and the floor was coated with clay. On a cot lay a mattress accompanied by two bolster pillows for comfort. A battery-operated TV with a video player was strategically placed by the side of the cot in such a way that one could only see the TV from a specific spot beside the cot. In one corner of the cot sat a locked box and a thick ledger book bound in red cloth. Nearby, the solitary wooden stool indicated that no seating arrangement for visitors had been made intentionally.

Ratnakar was sitting at the edge of the cot, angrily shaking his leg. As Jubed entered and stood, Banwari followed him. Before they could understand what was happening, Ratnakar suddenly sprang to his feet and said, "You want your money? Here – take this, take this," delivering two heavy slaps across their faces in rapid succession. The unexpected blows, in exchange for their desire to receive payment, left the two labourers utterly stunned, standing frozen in disbelief. Their hearts cried out in silent anguish, with unshed tears pooling at the corners of their eyes. But Ratnakar's anger didn't subside; he continued relentlessly, "If I had done this in front of everyone, would you have any respect left? And why don't you save up your money when you get paid? I run a business, not a charity. Now, get lost – get back to work."

Banwari's pained words slipped out naturally, "Let's go, Jubed brother. This pot too will break one day."

"What did you say? You think I'm a pot of sins? You'll break it, will you?" Ratnakar shouted, raising his hand to strike again, but Jubed stepped in between them.

With folded hands, he pleaded, "This is enough at our age, master. May Allah bless you."

"Go, get out. Blessings will come automatically." Ratnakar gestured dismissively, ordering them to leave. Overcome with financial distress and humiliation, the two helpless labourers, heads bowed, left the office and returned to their work.

Seeing Sandhya with bricks on her head, Jubed called out to her. She approached and asked innocently, "What happened, uncle?"

"Nothing, nothing. Haven't seen Damu since yesterday? If he were here, this wouldn't have happened."

Banwari added dejectedly, "Did Damodar quit his job?"

"No, uncle. He left the house this morning for work. He's the master of his own will. Only God knows where he is and what he's up to," As Banwari and Jubed walked away in another direction, Sandhya muttered these final words to herself while walking on.

***

In anger and sorrow, Damu had left the house

in the morning and, out of habit, came to the banyan tree and sat down under it. Leaning his sleepless, restless and tired body against the tree, he pondered over various thoughts keeping Puja in mind. Slowly, in the cool morning breeze, sleep began to claim his eyes.

***

In the outer room of her modest lower-middle-class home, Puja's voice, simmering with anger, came through, "No, never."

Standing in front of her, the over-thirty Bilton Singh, unfazed by her firm rejection to his unjust and vile proposal, retorted in a low voice, "Why 'no'? I am not that bad. Just say 'yes,' or else –"

This time, Puja's voice broke free of any restraint. "Or else what? You'll ruin my reputation?"

"No, no, that's not it," he began to say, but before he could continue, Puja's father, Badri Prasad, emerged from inside. Bilton quickly ending the old topic, forced a grin and muttered a brief, "*Namaste.*" Badri, with his unkempt white beard and heavy face, gave the impression of a man well-acquainted with liquor, his bloodshot eyes—an aftereffect of early morning drinking—

perfectly validating the 'drunkard' title Bilton had often bestowed upon him. The over-sixty Badri invited Bilton to sit and, struggling to keep his balance, first sat down himself in the wooden chair specially crafted for him. Sensing the moment was right, Bilton, more enthusiastic, repeated his greeting, "*Namaste*, Uncle."

The first "Namaste" probably merged with this second one and finally made its way into Badri's ears. "Yes, yes, sit down, my boy. Why are you standing?"

Glancing sideways at Puja, Bilton pretended to stammer awkwardly, "Yes, uh—no—I mean—what if someone here feels bad?"

Looking at the silent but clearly agitated Puja with an indifferent expression, Badri said, "Who would mind? No, no. You go inside—make some tea."

Puja stomped off without a word, her reaction ignored by Badri, who casually turned back to Bilton, "So, what's the news, my boy?"

Relaxing into his seat, Bilton began, "Uncle, I've come to talk to you. Please do not take it the wrong way, but about Puja— You don't really –"

Unable to find the right words from his vocabulary, Bilton suddenly, out of habit, blurted out, "*You not care*—yes."

Badri, having an inexplicable admiration for English despite his poor grasp of it, would feel overly pleased with even such broken sentences. His respect for the speaker would grow. Now, without admitting his ignorance, he responded, "Explain a bit more, son."

"Have you ever paid attention to her age? How old –"

"I understand, my boy—I understand everything. Three years ago, a match had come for her. I don't know what happened, but they backed out even after finalizing everything. Back then, her mother was alive. My only son got married in the city and stayed back as a '*gharjamai*' (live-in son-in-law). Unable to bear this pain, her mother, who was already plagued by various ailments, died of a heart attack. Even after I was left alone, I brought up the idea of marriage with Puja several times, but she dodged the topic every single time. I thought—"

"You thought – the girl is at her own home, so what's wrong in this? Since you live alone, you think this out of affection and a bit of self-interest. You're lost in the haze of your own intoxication, Uncle, and over there —" Billton deliberately paused with a crooked smile.

Badri picked up the thread and asked, "And over there, what?"

"And over there, your maid servant's son –" saying this part in a relatively lower voice, Bilton paused to gauge Badri's reaction. Badri's curious question came, "What happened to him?"

"Nothing much—" Billton's eyes sparkled with cunning. "I've given him a tight warning. The rascal was trying to get close to Puja." Billton said, tightening his jaws dramatically as he narrated the words, so engrossed in his story that he didn't notice when Puja had entered, carrying a tray with a cup of tea that had been prepared for him long before.

Puja, now fearless, slammed the tray with the cup of tea onto the table and, with fiery words, confronted Billton. "Why don't you talk about your own vile deeds? You go around preying on other people's mothers and sisters. Gambler! Disgusting!"

Unable to tolerate his daughter's harsh truth, Badri, wobbling as he stood up, swiftly slapped Puja hard across the face before Billton could stop him.

Sobbing, Puja seemed determined to finally speak her heart today. "Go ahead, slap me again. Kill me if you want, father. But know this—I love Damu. Yes, I do."

Rage and hatred seemed ready to explode from Bilton's furrowed eyes. Puja flung her final words at Badri, whose face was filled with anger and astonishment. "And – I will marry Damu."

But before Badri could raise his hand again, Bilton grabbed his arm. "No, Uncle. Let it go. She doesn't understand."

"Get out of my sight! You've disgraced me," Badri shouted at Puja.

Accepting her father's scorn, Puja walked straight out of the house.

Badri stood there, his lips twitching to one side and his brows furrowed, head bowed in a daze. His intoxicated mind slowly realized why his daughter's previous engagement had fallen apart and why she had avoided the topic of marriage ever since.

With a sly, satisfied grin, Bilton steadied Badri. "Uncle, forget it. These are just a woman's whims—'*that is right*'. I didn't take it to heart. You sit down." Guiding Badri to a chair, he continued, "What I actually came here to talk about has been left unsaid."

Badri had a lot of trust in Bilton. In the camaraderie of a tavern, initial trust often runs high. It's easy to see how quickly trust can be won over when alcohol is involved, as evidenced by Bilton Singh. It was this very trust that made Badri feel somewhat reassured, prompting him to inquire about Bilton's intentions.

Without wasting any time, Bilton quickly stated, "Uncle, there's only one way to escape this disgrace, and that's by marrying Puja off—to a good man."

"Who will marry her?" Badri asked, his voice tinged with disappointment.

In response to Badri's disheartened question, Bilton, without hesitation and with excessive humility, said, "Uncle, if you look my way – I –"

"Will you marry her?" Badri clasped his hands together in a gesture of prayer, clearly pleased.

"No, I mean—only if you like me—"

Bilton's cunning intention went unnoticed by Badri, who felt overwhelmed with emotion. "Son, you have eased my sorrow. You are indeed my choice—for my daughter."

With a smile of slyness creeping onto his face, Bilton pretended to be excessively humble reaching for Badri's feet.

Badri, now fully taken by emotion, seemed even more intoxicated. "That's enough, son. I bless you; may you both be happy. And from now on, we are father-in-law and son-in-law, friends." With that, Badri burst into hearty laughter.

Feeling a sense of ultimate triumph, Bilton joined in the laughter. Wanting to share this imagined happiness, Badri made a gesture with his index finger and thumb, "Then let's do it—one peg each. Shall I bring the bottle from inside?"

"No, Uncle—"

"No more 'Uncle.' Call me 'Father-in-law,' my boy."

"Alright, 'Father-in-law.' I won't have any now." Trying to mask his mischievous expression with a show of simplicity, Bilton added, "Why don't you come to Chatur Singh's 'Hangout' today? Our '*yaari*' (friendship) will truly blossom when there be together you, me and '*Vilayati Rampiyari.*'(foreign liquor)"

Both burst into laughter again—Badri in joy over the prospect of getting drinks, while Bilton celebrating his victory.

In Bihar and Uttar Pradesh, there was a special type of tea sold on trains, which they called '*Rampiyari.*' In jest, they nicknamed foreign liquor '*Vilayati Rampiyari*' after that tea. And Chatur Singh's '*Adda*' (hangout) was a local liquor bar where illegal foreign alcohol flowed alongside the performances of dancing girls. Needless to say, it was there that Bilton had first introduced Badri, who was used to drinking country liquor, to the taste of foreign alcohol.

"Well then, I'll take your leave now, Uncle—no, I mean, Father-in-law," Bilton chuckled as he reached the doorway without looking back. He extended one last invitation with a sly grin, "But do come. I'll be waiting for you there."

"I will come, of course, I will." Despite going against societal norms, Brahmin by caste, Badri

Prasad Pandey, nodded to himself in joy. Perhaps it was the thrill of his daughter's marriage being fixed or the excitement of having found a steady drinking companion that made him respond this way.

***

Bilton, in the guise of a monstrous demon, seemed to be dragging Puja away to some unknown destination. Her cries for help echoed like Sita's desperate pleas, 'Save me, save me!' in the clutches of Ravana, the antagonist of epic Ramayana. Hearing her distress, Damu ran at breakneck speed to save her, only to stumble on something as hard as stone and fall flat on his face, abruptly awakening from the nightmare. As he opened his eyes, he could see the sun nearly overhead through the gaps in the leaves. Despite summoning the strength of a determined mind to get up, his negative thoughts ordered him to stay seated. So, sitting there gloomily, he began to contemplate the past and the future together.

Whether it was due to Damu's willpower or Puja's own desire, she had already reached the other side of the tree. Since stepping out of her house, her heart, which had been breaking continuously, felt rejuvenated upon seeing Damu. With a smile on her face, she tiptoed forward, picked up a small pebble mischievously, and quickly threw it at Damu's back before hiding behind the tree. When Damu turned around and saw no one, he thought something had fallen from the tree and turned back again. This time, as Puja picked up another pebble and threw it, Damu, alert, turned around and spotted her, causing her to burst into laughter as she approached and sat beside him. In response to Damu's dry smile, she asked, "What happened? Are you still angry?"

"I'm not mad at you."

Puja mimicked his words and, playfully shaking Damu's chin, said, "Then why the long face?"

When Damu responded with another dry smile, Puja, holding her ears and making a funny face, said, "Forgive me for yesterday. I was scared, really."

"You easily said you were scared, but I couldn't sleep nor stay awake all night. I didn't even go to work."

"Why? Why didn't you go?"

"What's the point of going? I'm not going to get

paid anyway. You know, they still owe me three weeks' worth of wages. The owner's business is running just fine, but he just has no intention of paying us."

"So, what will happen if you don't go?" Puja asked softly.

"I didn't go today. Tomorrow someone else won't go. The next day, another person will refuse too—until, eventually, everyone stops going. The owner will be forced to pay up. I'll make everyone understand."

Listening intently, Puja playfully whispered the word 'rebellion,' which only fuelled the fire in Damu's already burning mind. He stood up, resolute, and declared, "Yes, I will rebel. If not for myself, then for others. I want to tear down this divide between high and low, rich and poor, from its very roots. If only I could—"

Interrupting him with a gesture of soft reprimand, Puja clasped her hands together, speaking in a gentle, almost playful tone, "Alright, alright, stop it, please. It's my fault. Calm down now."

Accepting her request, Damu gradually sat down, but continued speaking, "I get all tangled up inside my own mind. No one ever tries to understand me. You know well, at home, there's a bedridden, disabled, and ailing father whose medical expenses have become a heavy burden. My widowed sister works, too—at a brick kiln. My mother goes house to house, washing dishes. Yet still, they don't want me to go to the city. They say once someone goes to the city, they never come back. They end up staying there forever."

Each word sank deep into Puja's heart, filling her with sympathy for Damu. But those last two sentences hit her like a sudden blow, stirring an old, deeply buried pain within her. With tearful eyes, she muttered to herself, "It's not wrong. Look at my brother. After our mother died, he came back once – and now, maybe, he'll only return when our father dies—" Her voice choked up, unable to continue.

Damu gently took her hand in his, offering both sympathy and support. "Don't say that. Not everyone is the same. I want to go to the city, and I want to come back as well."

Puja, pulling herself together, slipped off the only gold bangle on her left hand and extended it towards Damu. "Take this. Sell it and buy medicine for your father. Give some money to the family, and use the rest to go to the city. If I keep it, one day it will surely end up in my drunk father's belly as liquor. But you must come back, no matter what." Her lips tried to form a faint smile, though her eyes didn't cooperate, allowing her tears to flow freely.

As a tear fell onto his palm, Damu smiled softly, his resolve shifting. He gently slipped the bangle back onto Puja's wrist and said, "That's it? This much courage? Well, now my plans to go to the city are completely cancelled." Making a mock gesture of repentance by crossing his hands over his ears and pointing with his eyes, he caused Puja to burst into laughter.

"Oh, stop it, I never actually objected. I just—" she began.

"You women, you're something else!" Damu interrupted with a loud, hearty laugh.

Seeing Damu laugh like that, instead of feeling happy, a sense of unease gripped Puja. She hadn't said anything for so long to avoid deepening Damu's worries, but no matter what his reaction might be, she couldn't keep such an important matter hidden from him.

Noticing the worried look on Puja's face, Damu stopped laughing, but Puja's vacant look remained unchanged. Damu snapped his fingers in front of her eyes, calling her name, which brought her back to reality. When Damu responded with a questioning look, she spoke solemnly, "That scoundrel came home today and frightened my *baba* (father). I don't know what he might do tomorrow."

Upon hearing this, Damu's brows furrowed in concern, and when Puja revealed what Bilton had said, Damu roared and sprang to his feet. "That bastard! I'll—"

Puja quickly stood up as well and stopped him, saying, "No, you won't do anything. *Baba* will surely tell me what happened after I left. Even if that shameless man proposed, *baba* won't agree so quickly. Let some time pass. Everything will be fine. You go home now, and make sure to go to work tomorrow."

With a nod reminiscent of a simple-minded boy, Damu moved forward.

"And remember about the city," Puja said, walking behind him.

Turning around, Damu noticed Puja's beautiful pink lips seemed to smile, as if wanting to say something else. Habitually, she had left her hair unbound today. In a sudden gust of wind from unknown, her waist long hair cascaded down, brushing against her graceful chest. Her silent, beckoning eyes seemed to call out to Damu. As the afternoon sun's glare enveloped him, Damu took Puja's hand and pulled her closer, longing to touch his lips to her anticipated ones, exchanging unspoken emotions in that moment. In a moment of unfulfilled desire, a familiar thrill suddenly coursed through Puja's entire body, causing her eyes to close and she felt as if the blazing sun in the open sky had been obscured by clouds. The brief wait now seemed to stretch into what felt like an eternity.

As Damu advanced for the second step in an attempt to satisfy the desire stirring within him, a familiar voice suddenly echoed from somewhere, like thunderbolts in a clear sky.

"Look here, while the elder sister is wilting in the scorching noon sun, the younger brother is cooling his hot youth by plunging into the ocean of love."

Damu's head spun as he noticed Bilton Singh's

two henchmen. He released Puja's hand and moved towards them. The thug-like henchman wasn't backing down and began advancing with menacing steps toward Damu.

"What's up? Have you forgotten about yesterday?"

In support of the thug's intimidation, the second henchman—part goon, part joker—chimed in mockingly, "Do I need to remind you again?"

"What are you planning to remind me of, you bastard?" Damu's voice barely finished echoing when Puja's words reached his ears. "Damu, teach them a lesson today. Don't let them go."

In an instant, Damu landed a solid punch on the hybrid character. Before the man could regain his balance or strike back, another punch followed by a swift kick sent the sneering fool crashing to the ground. Unsurprisingly, it was this joker who had made the sarcastic comment about 'hot youth' et cetera earlier.

As the second henchman advanced, Damu swung at him swiftly, but this one was more skilled and managed to counterattack. Fuelled by a desire for revenge from yesterday's incident, Damu delivered two quick punches straight to his opponent's face, causing blood to trickle from the man's mouth. Without giving him a chance to recover, Damu kicked him hard, sending him face-first into a nearby tree.

Seeing his stronger companion take a beating, the joker-like henchman scrambled away, crawling on the ground in a desperate attempt to escape. Watching him flee and realizing the gravity of his own situation, this second one also bolted, running for his life.

Puja waved her hand playfully, saying, "Well done! Well done!" as if to brush off the tension. Her light-heartedness brought a sense of calm to Damu. He ran both his hands through his tousled hair to fix it, before setting off with her down the dirt road toward home.

***

The stack of bricks above Sandhya's head offered her sweat-drenched face a temporary shade, even if for just a short distance. Ramdeen's gaze had wandered uncertainly for a while before it finally fell on Sandhya, who had slowed down from exhaustion. After glancing around, he made his way past the tall stacks of raw bricks and came up in front of her. Indulging in the sultry afternoon's lethargy, he ogled Sandhya's untended beauty and whispered suggestively, "Why do you work so hard, Sandhya? Why don't you rest a bit in some corner? I'll join you too—"

The combined heat of the sun and Ramdeen's unacceptable remark furrowed Sandhya's brow. A voice of utter annoyance escaped her lips, "Why do you keep pestering me? Go and do your own work."

Picking up one of the four or five bricks lying around, Ramdeen gestured with his eyes and replied, "That's exactly what I'm doing." Then he placed the brick onto the stack beside him.

Using her left hand to wipe the stinging sweat trickling from her forehead with the end of her *saree*, while supporting the weight of her head with her right hand, Sandhya continued arranging the bricks from the overhead stack onto the shelf in front, expressing her anger, "Yes, yes, I know just how much work you do and how you do it. In the morning, you disappeared after setting up Banwari uncle and Jubed uncle to squeeze your own wage out of them. God! What a mess you made of their lives! And you—"

Picking up another brick, Ramdeen interjected mockingly, "Why do you bother with other people's business and ruin your own head? Look—"

"I don't need you to show me anything—understand? And listen, if my brother even gets a hint of what you have in your mind, I swear, he will make things very difficult for you. Now get out of my way." With the bricks now arranged, Sandhya turned and walked straight away.

After a brief pause, Ramdeen raised the brick as if to place it on the stack but then dropped it to the ground instead. Staring at Sandhya as she walked away, he muttered under his breath, anger and regret mingling on his lips, "Look at her airs, the little madam!"

***

Lying on the bed, Hariram stared blankly at a corner of the bare room, probably trying to reconcile the discrepancies between his life's expectations and reality. His focus was broken by Raimoni's caustic remark as she entered through the inner door, holding a bowl of hot oil in the torn end of her sari.

"You're turning our son into a complete good-for-nothing. It's like he's sold his sense of shame at the market. His elder sister is sweating it out, and look at the young brother—talking nonsense and getting involved in useless affairs." As she said the last few words, she placed the bowl beside her husband on the bed, dipped three fingers into the hot oil, and began to massage his arm in long strokes.

"When a boy grows up, do you need to spell things out for him like you do—"

"Shut up. You're the one spoiling him. You sit around all day and now you're making him useless too." Raimoni's hands moved more vigorously as she continued the massage.

Hariram waved his hand in exasperation and said in one breath, "Your constant nagging has made my life unbearable. Leave me alone—I don't want any of this." He couldn't finish his sentence as a fit of coughs, tinged with a note of despair, overtook him.

"Of course, the truth will taste bitter to you. You say so easily, 'I don't want any of this,' but if it weren't for 'this,' would you still be alive?" Letting go of his arm, Raimoni began to massage his legs, bitterness seeping through her words. "It's you who is everyone's worry."

"Who wants to live this cursed life? Death would be better than—" Unable to finish due to the intensity of his coughing, Hariram shook his head, trying in vain to express what remained unsaid. His eyes, bulging under the pressure of the relentless cough, conveyed a mute, desperate appeal as he wheezed uncontrollably.

Startled, Raimoni shifted slightly on the bed, her hand trembling as she ran it over her husband's chest, her voice laced with fear as she tried to calm him. But Hariram brusquely brushed her hand away, his breath seemingly trapped in his chest. In an instant, regaining her composure, she leapt off the bed, hurried to the nearly empty medicine box, and grabbed the inhaler. Holding Hariram's head, she inserted the nozzle into his still-gaping mouth and pressed twice, only to find that the inhaler was finished. An involuntary gasp escaped her lips, "Oh God!" But noticing a faint relief on Hariram's face, she offered her first words of solace, "No, no, just try to calm down a little."

Hariram's eyes and forehead creased as he tried

to stifle the cough, his face almost on the verge of tears, seemingly wanting to say something, his expression tinged with a hint of resentment.

An unspoken reaction born of sorrow, shame, and worry made Hariram's eyes well up. He suddenly turned his face away and closed his eyes, while harsh-voiced Raimoni's tears trickled down her poverty-worn cheeks. Just then, the voice of their neighbor's young daughter, Munni, drifted in from outside. "Auntie, auntie."

Before Raimoni could wipe her tears with her saree, twelve-year-old Munni stepped in through the open door, her curious gaze trying to grasp the situation. Hariram, as if trying to suppress his cough, attempted to bring a smile to his face.

"What happened, auntie? Uncle seems unwell," Munni asked.

While Raimoni pressed the empty strips of the medicine box to find a pill, she addressed Munni's curiosity, "Yes, just now he started coughing."

Hariram, with a natural calmness interspersed with a cough, expressed his helplessness, saying, "Nothing much. A sick body always feels bad."

Bringing a glass of water in an old steel tumbler,

Raimoni approached her husband with a tone softer than usual, "Don't talk. You might cough again." Then, turning to Munni, she said, "Munni, go call your mother."

"She's the one calling you. That's why I came to tell you," Munni replied.

While feeding the tablet to Hariram, Raimoni said, "Alright, then you sit a little with your uncle. I'll quickly go and meet your mother."

Munni pulled the mat that was rolled up beside the bed and sat down, saying, "Yes, aunty."

After placing the glass in its proper place, Raimoni, deep in thought, hurriedly moved forward and soon saw Munni's mother approaching from the opposite direction. Though Munni's mother was two years older than Raimoni, her health and physique made her appear two years younger. However, the sari she wore suggested that their financial statuses were equal.

"It's good that you came, *didi*(elder sister)." Raimoni's anxious tone left Munni's mother a bit puzzled.

"Why? What happened?"

"Damu's father suddenly had a coughing fit. All the medicines are finished. *Didi*, if you have— I feel embarrassed to ask, but instead of asking outsiders, I thought I'd ask you, whom I consider my own—" Raimoni spoke in one breath and looked at Munni's mother, only to find that her eager eyes had dulled, and her closed lips now wore an expression of newly-bloomed despair.

"What happened, *didi?*" Raimoni asked curiously.

With a dry smile that matched the afternoon's aridity, Munni's mother expressed the cause of her despair, "No, nothing much. We've become slaves to our circumstances, reaching out to each other for help. I came to ask if Damu could request the shopkeeper to give us a few more things on credit. Everything at home is running short. I didn't want to mention it in front of 'devar ji' (brother-in-law)—so, anyway, let that be. You first get *devarji*'s medicines."

Raimoni hesitated, about to say something, but then, suddenly aware, she brought back her lost urgency and replied to Munni's mother's questioning gaze, "*Didi*, I left Munni with her uncle. Please look after everything and take care of him."

"Don't worry. I'm here; you go on."

"I'll be right back," saying this, Raimoni quickly disappeared into the narrow lane of the *Dalit* slum, her steps swallowed by the oppressive silence of the scorching afternoon.

Their brief exchange concluded as Munni's mother, walking towards Damu's house, murmured to herself, "Will this constant struggle of the poor ever end?"

***

About four miles, or roughly six and a half kilometers, away from Damu's village, on the outskirts of a small town (*Kasba*), Chatur Singh's country liquor den would usually come alive after dusk. But even at this odd hour, a couple of drunks could be seen, staggering around and slumping in semi-dark corners. The real action during the day, however, was gambling.

In front of the row of shops, a middle-aged man, bare-chested with long hair, dressed in a simple skirt and vermillion on forehead, was dancing while making small firecracker-like noises by whipping his bare back with a fake whip. His emaciated wife followed behind, incessantly scraping a stick on a small drum, producing a monotonous moaning sound as she begged—something commonly seen in Maharashtra and in some parts of Gujarat, where these performers are known as '*Kadaklaxmi*'. The sparse crowd of men and women, under the blazing afternoon sun, moved past them with little urgency, each preoccupied with their own destination.

From a distance, Bilton Singh, dressed in a colourful printed kurta over his pants, rode into Chatur Singh's den on a Bullet motorcycle. Needless to say, among his countless vices, gambling was no secret to anyone familiar with him, and his current attire clearly indicated that he was prepared for both gambling and the dancing girls' performance.

***

Badri was sitting in the outer room of his house, drinking without hesitation. His intoxication had risen well in tandem with the day's temperature. Lifting the bottle in front of him and feeling its weight, he realized it was empty. Gazing at the last poured peg in the glass, a sense of gloom seemed to wash over him. Just then, glancing out through the open door towards the gate by the road, a thrill ran through his drunken mind.

Seeing Sandhya's still preserved beauty and youthful figure swaying her hips as she walked closer, he emotionally murmured to himself, "Now, colour will fill my colourless life."

Seeing Sandhya walk straight inside through the open door, many imagined games of affection and kisses played in his mind. Just as he was about to embrace her, the long-ago impoverished and prematurely aged Raimoni, having lost her youth due to poverty, suddenly jerked away, stepping back.

"What are you doing, sir?"

As the veil of emotional delusion lifted from his wine-clouded eyes, he glanced at Raimoni, whose intense displeasure caused his face, forehead, and brows to contort in discomfort. Forgetting all the constraints of her dire situation, as the intense discomfort washed over her, the words of rebuke slipped from Raimoni's lips. "Shame on you, *babu*(master)! Have you sunk so low in the intoxication of alcohol?"

Sometimes, instead of Raimoni, Sandhya would come early in the morning to do the sweeping and washing, spending some time with Puja. During those moments, something would stir within

Badri's mind, but he always kept it to himself. Today, however, after this unintended incident, he still couldn't find the words to express it. Instead of feeling humiliated, his anger surged to its peak as his intoxication diminished.

"Yes, I am that low. So, what? But why have you come at this odd hour, knowing there's a drunkard in this house? Huh?"

"Compulsion of poverty brought me here, *babu*. This compulsion forces the poor to go anywhere at any time, *babu*."

"Just like the same way your son was forced to ruin my daughter? You come here under the guise of work, and then send your son after Puja? You people aren't poor; you're cunning." Whatever the underlying meaning was, Badri said these words out of anger, fuelled by Bilton's instigations earlier in the morning, and to hide his own present guilt.

Raimoni, eyes brimming with tears, avoided the topic and pleaded desperately, "Say what you will, *babu*. I came to ask for some money for my husband's medicine. Please give me some advance, *babu*. My husband's—"

"There'll be no money or anything. Get out of here. And listen—don't come to work from tomorrow." In his fury, half of Badri's intoxication seemed to evaporate.

"Please have mercy, babu—so harsh—"

"There'll be no mercy. And listen—" Perhaps Badri saw Puja approaching from a distance. He tried to make his words louder and clearer, "Yes—listen, tell your son never to—"

As soon as the topic of her son was brought up again, Raimoni wiped her tears and stood her ground. "That's enough, babu. A clap doesn't make a sound with one hand. Teach your daughter. Boasting about self-respect is very easy, but mastering one's nature is truly difficult, babu."

Puja had just stepped onto the threshold. Raimoni's words reached her ears completely.

Shaking his head and glaring at Raimoni, Badri warned, "Enough, stop the lecture and get out. I'll deal with my daughter and your son too. My buzz is completely ruined."

As Raimoni turned around, she saw Puja.

Raimoni's entire family knew about the

relationship between Damu and Puja. They had accepted it only because of Puja's persistence and had never spoken to anyone about it. But at this moment, Raimoni had no patience for a pleasant conversation with her. She tried to pass by, but Puja blocked her path.

"Wait, *kaki*(aunty). I have something to say. I told *baba*(father) this morning, and now I want to tell you—"

Raimoni's eyes were filled with disbelief. Badri stood with his mouth agape, astonished at his daughter's audacity.

"I love Damu, and Damu loves me. If we don't get married or if anything happens to him, I will kill myself."

Before Puja could finish, Raimoni had already crossed the threshold and was heading toward the gate, speaking loudly, "What could possibly happen to Damu? There's a fierce fire within him. It's just buried under the ashes of poverty. If that fire ever erupts, it will be a massacre. A massacre."

Before Raimoni's voice could fade away, Puja, standing outside the door, tried to say something, but Badri, grabbing her hand, pulled her back, saying, "You come inside," trying to drag her in. She screamed, "I will give my life – *kaki*, you hear me –"

Pushing her a little further inside, Badri steadied himself, slipped on the pair of shoes kept right beside the door, stepped outside, and locked the door from the outside. As usual, he was still wearing his kurta over the dhoti after his morning bath. From inside, Puja's sobbing voice could be heard, "– I love Damu –" Ignoring her, Badri, his eyes squinting against the sudden glare of the sun, staggered down the street, muttering to himself, "Stay locked inside. I have to figure something out for you."

Puja's helpless cries still echoed from within.

***

Hariram lay with his eyes closed on the bed. Below, Munni played with a few pebbles on the mat while her mother sat beside her, dozing off while lost in a world of fanciful thoughts. Suddenly, seeing Damu step just beyond the threshold, Munni exclaimed, "Brother is here!"

Hariram opened his eyes. Before Damu could

grasp the situation, Munni's mother stood up and stopped him, lowering her voice significantly, "Listen, your father – well, you come outside for a moment." Saying this as she went outside, Damu followed closely behind her.

"Listen, Damu, your father had a sudden coughing fit. That breathing machine or whatever it is—it's empty now. I gave him some ginger juice with salt. You know, home remedies work better than those foreign medicines. See, he's lying calmly now. But remember, he has a heart condition too, so get the medicine as soon as possible. Your mother's gone for the same reason. You go inside. I'll just check on my house for a bit."

After offering this unnecessary advice to increase her importance, Munni's mother headed towards her house. Damu came inside and asked Munni to leave, and as he looked at Hariram, the latter called him closer.

As soon as Munni left, Hariram said to Damu, "You sit next to me."

"You should rest, *bapu*(father)."

"I can only rest there now. Eternal rest."

"Don't say that, *bapu*. You lie down. I'll arrange your medicine."

Hariram stopped his son by holding his hand. "No, you sit. I'm fine now. I want to tell you a few things. Listen carefully."

Damu didn't protest any further.

"Keep the fire that burns in your heart calm. According to God's will, perhaps the poor have to endure more. But after this endurance, happiness will surely come. Staying calm is a significant test from the higher powers."

As he started to cough a little, Damu tried to stop him, but Hariram continued, "And rebellion, revolution—these are not meant for the benefit of the poor now. The rich and corrupt leaders reap the rewards. I was once like you. But see, now I'm lying in bed. Listen to your mother. She loves you very much. She wants you to go to work—earn some money. And with that, let the household run through the hardships. If God wills, everything will be fine. Her words may be bitter, but see how much she cares for us. She struggles so much for us. I don't know where she's running around for my medicine in this scorching sun." Pausing, he closed his eyes, and tears rolled down the corners of his eyes, trickling down the sides of his forehead.

Unable to hold back his emotions, Damu went into the inner room to wipe his eyes.

***

Coal tumbled from the truck with a heavy thud, landing in the empty space beside the brick kiln. Although the afternoon had waned, the sun's intensity had not diminished. Several women with coal-blackened faces were carrying coal in baskets on their heads. Sandhya also had the same duty at this hour. Not far away, three naked children were lying in the shade of a brick stack, sleeping. Other workers were busy with their respective tasks at a distance. Raimoni entered the brick kiln's boundary from this distant side. After scanning the surroundings for a few moments and not spotting Damu, she moved a bit forward when a familiar woman, covered in mud and preparing the soil, greeted her. "*Ram Ram* (namaste), *kaki.*"

"*Ram Ram.* Haven't seen Damu around?"

"He didn't come to work today. Why? What happened, *kaki?*"

"Nothing really. Where is Sandhya?"

The woman raised her muddy hand and pointed

in the direction where Sandhya was, saying, "Over there," and then resumed her work.

Surprised to see her mother approaching, Sandhya stepped forward and asked curiously, "What happened, Ma?"

"When will that boy ever get his head straight? Your father's health suddenly worsened. His medicine is all finished. I thought I'd ask him to arrange some money and bring the medicine. But —"

"I thought brother was at home. What will we do now, Ma?"

"If you can talk to your master and get some money, then —"

"Master? No, Ma, Banwari *kaka*(uncle) and Jubed *chacha*(uncle) got slapped this morning just for asking for money. If I go, the same thing might happen again—"

"I will go with you. I will beg, even fall at his feet. Come with me. The master will surely listen. If we don't get the medicine, something terrible could happen at any moment. Let's go." With these words, expressing her mental preparation in one breath, Raimoni herself first started towards the office room. Sandhya, having no other choice, followed her mother.

Ramdeen frowned as he saw them approaching from a distance. Jubed and Banwari were shovelling sand. Recognizing Raimoni, Jubed remarked, "Isn't that Damu's mother?"

Nodding, Banwari added, "Indeed. Something must have happened for sure."

***

Ratnakar Singh finished the accounting in his ledger, counted the notes, and, placing them into the cash box, locked it just as Raimoni entered the room. Turning his head, he caught sight of Sandhya's face behind Raimoni, darkened by coal dust but still strikingly beautiful. Ratnakar's eyes became wide and unblinking, his mouth fell silent, and his heartbeat started to race. But Raimoni's voice interrupted the moment.

"Master, I am Sandhya's mother."

Composing himself, Ratnakar shifted his gaze and replied, "Ah, yes – speak."

Raimoni glanced at her daughter and said, "You tell him."

The desire from earlier that morning stirred again in Ratnakar as he eagerly said, "Yes – yes, speak up. Whatever you want to say, just tell me openly."

Noticing her daughter's hesitation, Raimoni took the lead, "Master, Sandhya's father suddenly fell ill. He has been unwell for a long time, and now his medicine has run out."

Ratnakar clicked his tongue sympathetically, and Raimoni, emboldened by his reaction, finally voiced the plea she had prepared in her mind, "Please, master, if you could give us some money for the medicine."

Seeing Ratnakar's show of sympathy, Sandhya supported her mother's request, "Yes, master, my brother and I will work even harder."

Ratnakar, casting a lustful glance, responded with a sly remark, "And how exactly will you both work, 'brother and sister'? Your brother hasn't shown up for work for two days."

"I will send him. He will come from tomorrow. Please give me some money, master." Raimoni took the responsibility for Damu.

Cunningly, Ratnakar laid down his condition,

"Alright. I will give you the money, but only because his father has fallen ill."

Pointing towards Sandhya, he made the statement, to which Raimoni nodded in agreement

Looking slyly at the recently closed money box and smiling deviously, Ratnakar laid out his full condition, "But there is no money right now. Come and take it when the work is done in the evening."

"The evening is almost here, master."

Initially angered by Raimoni's plea, Ratnakar glanced at Sandhya and once again broke into a sly smile, presenting an irrefutable argument. "I told you! There's no money right now. Bilton will bring it. You can come and collect it after your work. Now go—get back to work. And listen—do not tell anyone about this money, okay?"

Raimoni reluctantly nodded to accept the condition and, looking at Sandhya, said in a despondent voice, "Let's go."

***

Ramdeen, Jubed, and Banwari watched from their

respective places as Raimoni and Sandhya walked along the narrow path made of brick pieces in the middle. Out of curiosity, Jubed stepped forward and asked Raimoni, "What happened, sister?"

"Her father's health suddenly took a turn for the worse. So—" Raimoni paused deliberately, and Jubed filled in the gap with his assumption, "So you asked for money, and the master said 'no.'"

Sandhya inadvertently chimed in, "He said that—" but Raimoni quickly redirected the conversation, "Yes, brother, the master indeed said 'no.'"

Jubed pretended not to understand, even though he did. He nodded to himself and walked off in another direction.

Raimoni, now very worried, said to Sandhya as they reached the main road, "I don't know where your crazy brother is wandering now, and I don't know if your master's gambler son Bilton will bring the money or not. But you need to get the money. Remember one thing—if anything happens to your father again today, he won't survive."

Tears welled up in her eyes as she spoke the last

words, and then she hurried away. Sandhya stood motionless for a moment before returning to her work.

***

In the outer room of Chatur Singh's den, an illegal gambling session was in full swing. There was hardly any fear of the police. Even if, every six or nine months, the higher-ups would send a team to raid, arrangements were made well in advance to handle such situations. Bilton Singh was a regular patron of both gambling and liquor at this den, making him somewhat of a 'respected' figure here. It is worth mentioning that this 'honourable' Bilton Singh was none other than the sole son of the 'illustrious' Ratnakar Singh. While many doubted if the name 'Bilton' had any real meaning, there was no such ambiguity about 'Ratnakar', which most people associated with the notorious bandit 'Ratnakar' of epic Ramayana. Although Bilton had inherited most of his father's traits and actions, he also possessed a few of his own unique vices.

Despite losing twice in a row, Bilton kept playing, unfazed by winning or losing. For him, the thrill of the game was what mattered. This time, instead of playing blind, he picked up his cards, examining them one by one. Just as he was about to reveal the third card, his two henchmen entered the room. Upon seeing them, Bilton muttered to himself, "Ah, my luck will turn now." Then, addressing them, he asked, "Where have you been all this time? And hey, Jagga, what happened to your face? Were you chasing after some girl or what?"

Jagadish, aka Jagga, who had been beaten up by Damu a while ago, stood there silently with a sullen face. His companion, known for his humorous nature, was Chhote Lal, aka Chhutku. Though his home was three villages away, he spent all his time with Jagga, day and night. People whispered that there was some sort of peculiar relationship between the two, as Chhutku often ended up drunk on Bilton's money and would sleep with Jagga most nights. What a family they had!

Chhutku smirked and said, "You can say that, *bhai ji* (brother)."

 "Shut up, you coward! You ran away with your tail between your legs, leaving me all alone," Jagga snapped.

As he focused again on revealing the mystery

of the third card, Bilton added, "Stop playing riddles, tell me straight."

This time, Jagga decided to display some bravery. "That bastard Damu is getting bolder, *bhai ji*. He dared to confront me head-on, glaring at me. So, I gave him a good thrashing."

Chhutku chuckled again, and Bilton, catching on, said, "I get it—how many punches landed, and what kind they were. Don't worry. Tomorrow, I'll handle him in front of everyone at the kiln and put him in his place. Now stop ruining the fun. Get to work."

Bilton's last remark was a subtle signal, hinting at the need to resort to some sly tactics in the game. After all, whenever he won, it was always through cheating. It seemed like winning dishonestly was his fate, perfectly aligning with his character.

Without further ado, his two companions settled at a convenient distance, and the three-card illegal gambling session continued in full swing.

***

Along the narrow path they had made themselves, around thirty to forty paces apart on both sides, stood eighteen small houses belonging to the

Dalit slum. Nearby, a newly constructed two-storey house was in the process of having a television antenna installed on its roof—a simple aluminium stick antenna. Although satellite TV was supposed to be available in the area, it hadn't started yet. The owner of the house, who had adopted the name Lal Singh, was said to have come from a *Dalit* background, according to local gossip. Until about a year ago, he had worked at the brick kiln and lived in a small house, much like the others in the slum. His sudden wealth raised suspicion, and few believed he had come by it through honest means.

Just as she reached her small hut, slowly walking along the narrow path that the slum dwellers used, burdened by countless worries, Raimoni saw Damu sitting next to Hariram. The sight seemed to ignite all her tangled thoughts into fiery outbursts. "Where have you been? Just remembered your home now, did you? Where were you roaming? Do you have no shame? Your father is on the brink of death, and your poor old mother is running from door to door, banging her head in despair—"

"Ma, please, stop it. *bapu*—"

"Why should I stop? You're so worried about

your father now? You came home wandering around like a good-for-nothing. Does it hurt if I say something?"

Before Damu could say anything, Hariram chimed in sarcastically, "You've started again?"

"Yes, yes, of course, for you it's always 'started again,' right?" Raimoni retorted sharply, casting a scornful glance at Damu. "Look over there—Lal Singh's house got a TV now. They didn't even have a radio till yesterday. He works and earns money, makes progress, unlike you—"

Damu raised his hand in protest. "Ma, why do you always target me like this?"

Hariram pressed down on his son's hand with his left hand, signalling him to stop. But Damu's voice grew louder in self-defence, "What crime have I committed? I just didn't go to work for two days. If I had gone, would I have brought back the Taj Mahal? How can a man earning just two and a half hundred rupees a week dream of anything? And especially when three weeks' wages are still pending? There's just one kiln here, no factories, no other real chance for income. And, Ma, you're talking about Lal Singh, right? Well, listen—if everyone starts doing what Lal Singh does, not only will every house have a TV, they'll have guns as well. And then every person will live in fear of when someone will pull the trigger. We'll all be trapped in a world of oppression."

Raimoni stood frozen, a look of discomfort etched on her face.

Hariram coughed slightly and said, "Now, calm down, son."

"No, I won't calm down, and I won't stay in this village anymore. Whatever it is, I've studied a little. Even people who can barely sign their names are going to the city and earning four times more than us. Why am I stuck here? For Ma. I've been crushed under this poverty. *Bapu*, I cry alone seeing your condition," Damu said, his frustration spilling out.

Hariram tried to say something but couldn't. It seemed his asthma was acting up, though no one noticed. Damu continued, looking at Raimoni, "Not anymore. I'll go to the city now. I'll make something of myself. Only then will your constant taunts stop. Let me go, Ma – that's all I ask!"

Tears welled up in Damu's eyes. Raiomni noticed the sudden pause in her husband's breathing, his mouth open as he struggled for air. "What happened?" she exclaimed, immediately rubbing her hand across his chest. Wiping away his blurry eyes, Damu hurriedly placed the empty pump to his father's mouth and pressed it three or four times, urging, "Breathe, *bapu*. Look, I've stopped talking. I won't say anything more."

Raimoni also promised, "Yes, I won't say anything more either. You just stay calm."

Whether it was because of the small amount of medicine left in the inhaler or due to a psychological effect, Hariram gradually regained control. Damu helped him drink a little water.

Seeing her husband stabilize, Raiomni calmly told her son, "Damu, the afternoon is slipping away. Go to the kiln. The master has promised to give Sandhya the money. You take the money from her and head straight to the medicine shop. The doctor's note is in the medicine box."

Though Damu felt a bit doubtful about the master's promise to pay, he said nothing and quickly took the prescription from the box and left. Once her son had gone, Raimoni turned her full attention to her husband.

***

Despite losing quite a bit of money in the first two rounds, once his two cronies joined in with their usual trickery, Bilton's losses were not only recovered but more than doubled. In his excitement, he and his companions claimed a corner table at the bar early on, drinking heavily. Now, lost in intoxication and emotion, Bilton was openly revealing the dark side of his inner thoughts with a grand flourish.

"Look—damn, isn't this alcohol such a strange thing? Just two pegs, and everything turns colourful. So many vibrant dreams come to mind. I'll run in the elections. I'll win by making everyone drink. I'll open liquor shops and bars in every village. Damn, you'll see drunks in every house then. And then, money! I'll get contractors to dump a few truckloads of dirt and stone in the name of building roads, pocket the rest—money in the name of bringing electricity, stealing high-voltage wires, more money—just money, you get it?"

Jagga, as if he had just received a large share of money, downed half his glass in one go and rubbed his face arrogantly. However, the lingering pain from Damu's punch suddenly resurfaced, and the words he was about to say were buried deep inside him.

Chhutku, being his usual self, shrugged his shoulders along with his head, and out of sheer curiosity, asked, "But what if the public finds out—then what?"

"Ah, you fool—damn it! The public won't know anything. And if they do, they won't say anything. And if one or two do dare to say something, show them a stick or a gun, and they'll shut up. And if they don't, then—eliminate." Bilton ran his right hand across his neck to signify the word 'eliminate' and then supported himself by saying, "*That is right.*"

Jagga's sarcastic intelligence surfaced as he remarked, "*Bhai ji*, what other schemes— I mean, plans—are there?"

"Ha-ha. 'Scheme'—you got it right, you scoundrel. The next plan will be marriage—with Puja."

A voice from the outside counter floated in: "Give me a half of Bagpiper please."

Bilton suddenly paused after hearing the voice and quipped, recalling an old TV advertisement, "'One's Bagpiper, and we're the three peers'. That voice sounds familiar." Gesturing to Chhutku to go check, Bilton resumed his previous topic, saying, " Not later, the marriage will come

first—I'll break that damn woman's arrogance!
—"

Chhutku staggered back, and in a manner befitting his character, excitedly said, "*Bhai ji,* our future sister-in-law has a very long life—"

Bilton, intrigued, slammed his glass down on the table and stared at him with curiosity.

Chhutku completed his half-finished sentence, "—The moment you mentioned her name, her father just showed up!"

Jagga let out a sly chuckle, but Bilton snapped at him, "Shut up, you fool! I just took her name, and she didn't show up, yet you're talking about her long life— What? What did you say? Her father's here!" As the words from Chhutku finally sank in, Bilton, on shaky legs, rushed out.

At the outside counter, the young salesman asked for two hundred rupees, and Badri suddenly realized that in his rage, he'd forgotten to bring the money. Without hesitation, Badri admitted the truth, "I don't have any money today."

"Then, uncle, don't drink today," said the salesman, swiftly pulling back the bottle he had taken out towards himself while eyeing Badri, trying to gauge whether he was telling the truth.

"I'm a regular customer," Badri defended himself with a lie.

"You'll get the goods only if you pay, uncle. Everyone here is a regular customer. That's just how it is with alcohol."

By this time, Bilton had reached the counter and decided to assert his dominance over the young salesman. "What's this? You're asking my father-in-law for money? Shameless idiot! Useless fool! *'That is right'*," After spouting these epithets, he almost snatched the bottle from the counter. Then, flashing a sly grin of triumph towards Badri, he continued with mock hospitality, "I am honoured you've come, father-in-law! Why don't you come inside?"

Expressing his gratitude, Badri followed Bilton inside, who then loudly and joyfully shouted, "Hey, pour a peg for my father-in-law!"

The young man, though accustomed to witnessing numerous oddities in his career, stood momentarily stunned, watching Bilton walk away before returning to his work.

***

As the work came to an end, the kiln workers washed their hands and feet, preparing to head home. Some were changing into the pants and shirts they had hung up earlier. A few wrapped neatly folded mufflers around their necks, combing their hair, humming songs from a recently screened film as they walked, momentarily forgetting all their sorrows, poverty, and fatigue.

Just as Sandhya slowly began walking towards Ratnakar's office, a distant voice of a woman called out, "*Didi*, aren't you going home?"

"No, you go. I'll come later," Sandhya replied without stopping, her mind focused on Ratnakar's instructions.

Ramdeen, who had been observing for a while, suddenly stepped in front of her and blurted out, "Why aren't you going home now?"

"What's it to you?" Sandhya stopped and responded.

"Nothing, nothing to me. Just... your mother had come, right? And then you all went to the master... so, I was just—"

"So what? Do you need to know everything? Are you some kind of detective? Stop poking your nose into my business," Sandhya snapped back.

Ramdeen gritted his teeth and sneered, "One day, you'll see where this arrogance of yours gets you. I know you're going to get money. Good—if you get money today, we'll get ours tomorrow. Yeah, yeah, go on—just go."

Acknowledging the uncomfortable truth in Ramdeen's rude comment, Sandhya kept her head down and moved forward without responding.

***

Slanting from the cot, peeking through the window made from uneven bricks stacked like a grille, just about a foot above the ground, Ratnakar saw Sandhya approaching. With a sly grin, he then raised the volume a bit more than a whisper, of the foreign obscene film playing on the video player. The scene had just reached the beginning of an especially long sequence, which triggered a memory for him. The first time he had shown a bit of this very scene to Ramdeen's wife, she had almost perfectly imitated the rest of it with him. Ratnakar had thoroughly pleased himself by manipulating every part of her as he desired, rendering himself completely exhausted and although later he deducted thirty rupees on various pretexts, in the heat of the moment then, he had placed a full fifty-rupee note into her hand.

This morning, the very parts of Sandhya's body that he had longed to gaze upon filled his mind with vivid imaginations, and soon an irresistible surge of lust overtook him. Despite the turmoil within, his outward display of restraint was commendable.

As Sandhya entered the room, she saw her master sitting at the corner of the bed, watching TV. Though the scene wasn't visible from where she stood, just a couple of feet away, the sounds she heard left her feeling uneasy. There was no doubt that the spiritual practice of morning and evening prayers had instilled a sense of purity in both her body and mind.

Ratnakar, despite his overwhelming desire to possess Sandhya, pretended not to notice her presence. In the same manner, Sandhya, determined to avoid any attention from him, feigned deafness, bowing her head in silent prayer. "Master, could you please give me the money?" she requested.

When Ratnakar did not respond, Sandhya repeated, "Master," which finally drew his attention and he responded.

"Uh – oh – you've come."

"Yes, master. You said you would give me the money."

Instead of responding to Sandhya's desperate plea, Ratnakar gave a sly, lustful smile and poetically said, "Yes, must I give it to you as I promised you. So, I must keep my word for you. Come this side – here – watch this movie – it's really good. Come on."

With a trembling voice, even more ashamed, Sandhya, without looking anywhere, pleaded sorrowfully, "Please give me the money, master. It'll get dark before I can reach home."

"That's even better. You'll be going in the dark; no one will see you. Come closer. I'll give you your full salary, even more than that. You can take care of your father's treatment properly. I'll increase your brother's wages too. Just come once—"

Reaching the peak of his desire, Ratnakar's tongue grew stiff, making it difficult for him to finish his sentence. Unable to say anything more, he crouched down and suddenly grabbed Sandhya's hand with a forceful grip.

For a moment, Sandhya's body and mind transcended all obligations. With a sharp tug, she freed her hand and exclaimed, "What are you doing, master? I am like your daughter. You are the same age as my father!"

Ratnakar, struggling to maintain his balance, had to quickly plant his feet on the ground. A mixture of lust and anger boiled within him, and a suppressed fury escaped his lips, "Once a woman is of age, the difference in years shouldn't matter—so say the scriptures. Understand? And listen—if anything happens to your father, don't you dare blame me. Only blame yourself."

As a reaction to the silent tears rolling down Sandhya's face, the flame of anger within Ratnakar was instantly extinguished, while his lust surged again. Grabbing her hand, he pulled her closer, saying, "Forget everything, just come here once."

Like the vanishing warmth of the distant, setting sun, Sandhya's dwindling resolve seemed to fade. Her body slackened. The faint murmur from the television, Ratnakar's lustful, rasping voice, the birds chirping as they returned to their nests outside—all became an eerie silence, transforming into the sorrowful cries of the helpless Raimoni, echoing through Sandhya's ears, into her brain, and down to her heart, creating an indescribable pain.

'... *If something happens to your father again today, he won't survive.*'

***

As he walked on with a heavy heart, seeing the sun rapidly disappear beyond the horizon, Damu quickened his pace. Up ahead, he saw a group of workers approaching. As he passed them one by one, he caught sight of Jubed and Banwari, who had fallen behind. Surprised and curious, Jubed, startled by Damu's unusual appearance at this time, asked why he was out so late. Without breaking his stride, Damu replied frankly, "*Chacha*, my father's health suddenly worsened. I'm going to get money for his medicine."

Ramdeen, who had passed by earlier, suddenly turned around and sarcastically remarked, "Yes, yes, you'll get your money for sure. Go on, see how much your accounts have progressed in the dark with your sister."

Like a tree suddenly springing back upright after being bent by a gust of wind, Damu, with his broken spirit, rushed forward and attacked Ramdeen.

Ramdeen, too, had advanced with a roar, but before anyone could separate them, Damu managed to land a few punches and kicks. After quite a bit of shouting and commotion, Jubed calmed Damu down, saying, "We needed the money just as much, son. But that man slapped us instead of paying. Go now, check on Sandhya *bitiya*(daughter)."

Without any further delay and with an overwhelming sense of impending doom, Damu rushed towards the brick kiln.

***

After putting on his *kurta*, Ratnakar opened the box and took out all the money. He pulled out three crumpled hundred-rupee notes and handed them to Sandhya, who stood there lifeless, like a statue, with dishevelled hair and a rumpled sari, staring blankly. "Here, take it," he said. But before Sandhya could even close her fist around the notes, Ratnakar swiftly snatched one of them back with his right hand, leaving her with a fifty-rupee note from the remaining bundle. As if he was giving her something extra, he said again, "Yes, take this too. Keep it. Now go. And whenever you need money, just come like this after work.

You've won me over!" Finishing with that, he shoved the rest of the money into his pocket and let out a self-satisfied, nasal laugh, baring all his teeth.

The final words didn't quite register with Sandhya, who had just lost everything for a mere two hundred and fifty rupees—one-third of her rightful money. However, in the dimming twilight, Ratnakar's laugh appeared to her as the cruel cackle of a monstrous hyena emerging from the underbrush beneath the tall trees in the distance, like a heartless demon.

***

As soon as Damu reached the path leading to the brick kiln, he came face to face with Sandhya, dishevelled, clutching money in her fist. Perhaps due to the fading light of the dusk and the encroaching darkness of night, he couldn't notice the money in her hand and the tears streaming down her cheeks, but he instantly sensed the grim indication of something terrible that had just happened to his beloved elder sister. Without a word, Sandhya glanced at her brother once and continued walking her path. The fierce rage that had suddenly ignited in Damu's heart propelled him toward Ratnakar's office without allowing for any conversation. Even though Sandhya turned to stop her brother, the unspoken desire that had just awakened within her didn't let her do so. From the depths of her shattered heart came a silent cry, "May that demon be damned."

***

Locking the box and pocketing the key, Ratnakar adjusted his *dhoti.* Hearing the rapid, heavy footsteps, he looked up and instantly recognized Damu. Under the fading light of dusk, Ratnakar, like a demon in human form, failed to remember the fearsome incarnation of *Narasimha*, the mighty avatar of Lord Vishnu. Yet, in that moment, there was no doubt—he found himself face to face with *Death* itself, the embodiment of *Yama.* Without any pretense and as hastily as possible, he blurted out, "I will take full responsibility for your entire family—"

Before Ratnakar could say anything more, Damu lifted him and slammed him to the ground, kicking him relentlessly making him roll around. Responding to Ratnakar's earlier words, Damu furiously continued, "And you'll keep tormenting all the other families. Slapping someone in broad daylight—"

"Listen to me –"

"And call someone alone to give them money in the quiet of nightfall, ruining their life, right?"

"Let me go—let me go—I made a huge mistake—" Ratnakar couldn't finish his sentence. He could only groan in pain. Another kick sent him crashing face-first into his television, shattering it to pieces.

In a frenzy of rage, Damu tightened his grip around Ratnakar's throat, growling, "You'll never make another mistake. Never again. A scoundrel like you should be killed right in the middle of the crossroads. You have no right to live." Panting, he spat out the words with fury, grinding them through his teeth, all the while increasing the pressure on Ratnakar's already grievously injured throat. But when he failed to sense any response from Ratnakar, who had already died, Damu loosened his grip. Overcome with profound sorrow, anger, and shock, he let go, and Ratnakar's limp, lifeless body glided down, scraping against Damu's legs before falling to the ground.

As consciousness returned, Damu's eyes clouded over, and the images of his gasping father, helpless mother, and finally his raped sister rose before him, twisting his heart in anguish. In that moment, unable to discern what he should do, he stepped out of the sin-laden, oppressive office and vanished into the darkness of the back street.

***

As on many occasions before, Ratnakar had once again devised an excuse to send Munim outside with two tasks, ensuring that he wouldn't return before nightfall. At this moment, as he entered through the front of the brick kiln, Munim felt as if someone had slipped out through the back street.

"Who's there? Who's leaving?" he called out, guessing at the shadows. But no answer came. Only the distant sound of music from the radio of Debnarayan aka Debu, the lone resident labourer from another distant village, floated in the air.

Out of suspicion, Munim stepped into the wide-open office room. Sensing something ominous, he fished out the matchbox from his pocket, took out a matchstick and struck it. As the flame flared, a mumble escaped his lips, "Hey—look here—look at the master—" With the lit matchstick scorching his hand, he dashed out, stumbled in the dark, and scrambled on all fours like a monkey towards Debu's small room, collapsing with a thud on the narrow three-foot-wide porch. Breathless, he exclaimed, "Hey, *Deba*(further distorted nickname of Debu)—bring the hurricane lamp, quickly!"

Without even turning off the radio, Debu came with the hurricane lamp in hand and asked, "What happened?"

"Quiet, don't shout. Come, to the office room," Munim said, gathering himself a bit.

***

Rushing into the office room, Debu's blood ran cold at the sight. Steadying himself with the hurricane lamp, he placed both a question and a suggestion before Munim. "What should we do now? We should inform the owner's family."

Old Munim, having seen and heard much in his life, tucked the matchbox he had clutched in his left fist back into his pocket and shook his head in a low voice, "No, this is a murder case. The police will come. There'll be a lot of questions. We'll both get dragged into this. No, I'd better call Bilton." Squinting his eyes in thought for a moment, he added, "I think I saw someone fleeing. Did you see anyone?"

"Yes, I saw... Sandhya was leaving and—"

"Say it, damn it! And what?"

"*Munim ji*, Damu—yes, Damu was coming in and—"

"Damu! Damu did this! You pig, why didn't you follow him?"

"Munim *ji*, he went towards the office. And you know the master didn't like anyone keeping track of comings and goings. Especially around dusk—"

As Debu began to reveal the secrets he knew about Ratnakar, Munim, his accomplice, quickly cut him off. "Alright, that's enough. Keep your mouth shut now." With that, Munim pulled out the mobile phone Ratnakar had given him, found Bilton's name, and pressed the 'call' button.

***

Bilton, already soaked in alcohol, had also gotten Badri drunk to his throat. To heighten the excitement for Badri's first-ever dance performance, Bilton teased him, "Today Sheela *Bai* will dance, dear father-in-law. Your 'heart' will be pleased!" Before he could say more, the music started. Everyone's eyes were glued to the entrance, eagerly awaiting Sheela Bai's grand entrance. Just then, Bilton's phone rang in his pocket.

"Who the hell is it, messing with my fun?" he slurred, dragging his words, not bothering to lift his eyes from the doorway where Sheela Bai was about to appear. Fumbling around in his pocket, he cut the call without even checking. Then, with his hand out of his pocket, he blew a kiss into the air and playfully tossed it toward the mediocrely pretty dancer, clad in a low-quality *ghagra-choli*. But before he could relish the moment, the phone rang again.

"Who the hell are you, idiot? Do you have a *'chamiya'*(playful woman) like this at your place that I should even bother to answer your call? Damn you!" The blaring sound of the Bollywood 'item' song, the dancer's bare midriff, and her barely covered chest, combined with her provocative rhythmic gyrations, had Bilton so mesmerized that in his drunken stupor, he mumbled these words. Without bothering to check who was calling, he completely shut off his phone. Swaying to the music, he grabbed the glass of alcohol from the table with his left hand and began dancing to the beat.

Shameless Badri, in awe of his son-in-law's behaviour, shot Bilton a glance full of admiration thinking he would never find another like him and then turned his lustful gaze back to the dancer. Meanwhile, the two henchmen, already standing, clutched their glasses and, along with others in the room, started whistling and dancing, fully caught up in the moment.

***

As Munim pocketed the phone, he responded to Debu's questioning look, "First, he cut the call, and now it seems he's switched off the phone. I know exactly where he'll be now. Lock up here and give me the key. Then go to your room and keep your mouth shut." After a brief pause, his suspicious gaze returned. "No, you will come with me as well. Leave the hurricane lamp in your room, we'll take a torch. Hurry up."

As Munim walked out, Debu grabbed the lock and the key from the corner, locked the door, and handed the key to Munim. He then placed the hurricane lamp in his room, turned off the radio, and grabbed the three-battery torch Ratnakar had given him, joining Munim for the next move.

***

Coming through the darkness, Sandhya hesitated at the threshold of her home. She stood silent and still, clutching the folded notes in her hand, as if seeking forgiveness from the household deity before daring to enter. Raimoni, holding the lantern with its chimney blackened at the top, came forward. After raising the light and looking her daughter up and down, she instantly understood everything. She pulled Sandhya inside and shut the door.

"What have you done! Oh God! Was this the last thing left for us? How will we ever show our faces to anyone now? Did you not think, even once? Oh God!" Placing the lantern on the ground Raimoni lamented, clutching her head in despair. Her grief echoed in the room as Hariram listened in anguish. His vision blurred, and alongside the crumpled notes in her fist, Sandhya's entire form blurred before him. Overwhelmed by disbelief, hesitation, disgust, shame, and fear, as if he wanted to scream, " Sandhya, what more sin have you punished me with, you cursed one?"

But as soon as he uttered the name "Sandhya," a deep sorrow rose from his heart, causing his voice to choke. With an unbearable, intense pain in his chest, his eyes seemed ready to burst forth. The dim flickering light of the lantern seemed to spread like a current of darkness all around.

In an instant, Raimoni felt as if Hariram's long-disabled right hand seemed to stir slightly as his left hand clenched the bedsheet with pain and discomfort. But before Raimoni could grasp what was happening, Hariram's body became still, ending all his pain and suffering.

Responding to the unspoken signal of her heart, Raimoni shook her husband gently, her voice breaking with a muffled cry of despair. She wailed, calling out the name of her only absent son, "We are ruined, Damu! Look, your father has left us."

Tears streamed down her cheeks as Sandhya, who had made a futile sacrifice, bowed her head at her father's feet and wept uncontrollably.

***

Running lost and disoriented through the dark, Damu came to a sudden stop beneath the old banyan tree on the silent bank of the pond. This place had always offered him solutions to his problems, calming his restless mind time and again. But today? Why wasn't the storm inside him settling? As these thoughts swirled in his head, an unfamiliar wave of mixed anger, sorrow, and guilt overwhelmed him, and he burst into heart-wrenching sobs.

***

On the far end of the field, Munim walked steadily with the torch in hand, heading down the straight road that led to the small town or *kasba*. Debu followed closely behind. Munim's mind was a whirl of thoughts—many fears intertwined with numerous questions, and he was trying to piece together a combination of logical and illogical solutions. He took brief pauses as he rambled on about the vices and virtues of Ratnakar and Bilton, his own integrity, past incidents, and the possibilities of the near future. But the more Munim spoke, the deeper Debu's doubts grew. As they crossed the turn near Jubed's neighborhood, Munim abruptly said during a brief pause, "If we find a rickshaw at the school junction, we can make it a bit quicker."

Just moments ago, Debu had been responding with occasional small 'yes' and 'hmm', but now, hearing nothing, Munim turned around to find that Debu was no longer there. His heart skipped a beat in the thick darkness. Mustering his courage, he shone the torch around, and in an irritated voice, he shouted, "Hey, *Deba*! Where the hell did you go, you idiot?" Receiving no reply, Munim decided that reaching Bilton was far more urgent than looking for Debu. With a dismissive comment, he resumed his pace, muttering, "That coward probably ran off to drink *taari* (mild alcoholic drink – toddy) out of fear."

***

It wasn't a lie that Debu used to drink *taari*. After all, a little *taari* and *bhang* was somewhat justified for someone whose wife had run away branding him as an impotent and who had been forced to leave the village to save face. But in this terrifying situation, thoughts of *taari* hadn't crossed his mind at all. While gradually lingering a bit behind, as they reached the turn near Jubed's neighbourhood, Debu quietly slipped to the left, listening to Munim's voice grow distant, and hastily made his way into the darkness. He quickly reached the road beside the secret drinking den inside a hut with flimsy fences on the side of the road. Suddenly, someone unknown staggered out from the den and collided with Debu. The man, reeking of a pungent mix of toddy, *bidi*, and *khaini*, leaned in close, his bloodshot eyes nearly pressing against Debu's face. With a drunken slur, he bellowed, "Who's this? Debnarayan, is it?"

Debu felt a chill run down his spine. Munim probably hadn't gone too far yet. Without giving any answer, he cut off. The drunk man, realizing this, took his own path in the opposite direction and muttered to himself, "No? But it sure seemed like Debnarayan. Damn it, old fool! Curse it, the toddy's got quite a kick!"

Unhindered, Debu now reached Jubed's house.

***

Jubed Ali Khan, a devout Muslim and a widower, had married the daughter of a distant aunt out of love when he was a 20-year-old young man almost 38 years ago. After losing two sons in succession, he had a daughter. He had consulted various *qazis*(Islamic judges) and *fakirs* (spiritual leaders)who told him he wouldn't have the blessing of a son. Despite his wife's consent, his love for her was so profound that he never remarried. Their daughter was the same age as Sandhya and was her friend too. In fact, before the government built the *Dalit* settlement, Hariram used to live in this very village, and he had a deep friendship with Jubed. After his marriage, Jubed had considered Raimoni his sister, but from childhood, Sandhya called him *chacha* (paternal uncle), which everyone accepted. Later, Damu started addressing him the same way.

After two divorces, five years ago, Jubed's beloved daughter Rabeya had eloped with an elderly man from another village, taking her two daughters with her. A year later, Jubed's wife passed away due to gastric ulcer and jaundice. In the grief of his wife's loss, the once jovial and robust Jubed suddenly seemed to age overnight. Three years ago, a letter arrived with news of Rabeya's well-being. She was living in the suburbs of *Nawabs'* city, Lucknow, with her family. She had managed to send her daughters to school and even had a son. Jubed wrote several letters to the address she had provided over the course of a year but, receiving no response, eventually stopped writing. Now, he was completely alone, with only his brick kiln and his house.

As usual, after eating and dimming the hurricane lamp, Jubed was listening to songs on the radio when a frightened Debu quietly entered. Exhausted from the day's work and with a full stomach, Jubed had dozed off while listening to the music, so he didn't notice Debu's entrance. The moment Debu turned off the radio, Jubed slowly opened his eyes, surprised to see him. Before he could utter a word, Debu, without any preamble and in a subdued voice, told him the whole story and then said, "There's no doubt that a terrible thing has happened to Sandhya. I hold Damu in high regard, and I know you consider him like your son. That's why I'm bringing you this news before I leave."

"But where are you going?"

"I don't know. But I don't want to get involved in this mess, uncle. I'm just leaving,"

After saying this, Debu stepped down from the veranda and paused for a moment in thought. Resolving to sever the ties to his village and the bonds of his joint family, he decided to take the shortcut to the railway station through the fields from the school crossroad. Filled with fear, Debu then set off, determined yet deeply unsettled.

***

As usual, not finding any rickshaw at the school square, Munim walked to Chatur Singh's den. The singing and dancing were still in full swing.

Toward the end of each song, a few drunks would stagger onto the stage, dancing and throwing currency notes in a poor imitation of the Mumbai (earlier Bombay) style. The only difference lay in the value and volume of the notes. In Mumbai, the dancers were showered with hundred, five hundred, and thousand-rupee notes—generous sums. Here, it was ten- and twenty-rupee notes—meagre offerings. Yet, even from these small amounts, the *bai-jis* (dancers) earned a good commission. With graceful movements, the dancers collected the notes while performing, tucked them away into rented costumes, and after a brief break changing their outfits and hairstyles, resumed their dance. On special nights, when more high-profile *bai-jis* were hired, there were even occasional glimpses of fifty- and hundred-rupee notes fluttering down.

But today was no special occasion. So, Bilton, clutching a few twenty-rupee notes, swayed unsteadily under the influence of liquor, spinning and tossing each note while attempting to touch the dancer. From a distance, Badri, sitting at a corner table completely intoxicated, stared at the scene with lustful eyes, silently blaming his financial state for missing out on such indulgences. Jagga and Chhutku were in a similar state, but they remained seated, lazily swaying their bodies to the rhythm like many others, exhibiting drunken gestures. As the dancer retreated backstage, Bilton also descended from the stage with the others. Another song began playing at a relatively lower volume—it was the dancer's 'break', a brief intermission.

Munim scanned the room, spotting Bilton under the colourful lights of red and blue paper-wrapped electric bulbs, remnants from the old video hall days. He hurried over to him and, in a low voice, began an almost staged, artificial sob, "*Chhote Malik* (Young Master), a disaster has struck."

Barely paying attention, Bilton, still swaying from the drink, staggered toward his table. In response to Munim's repeated words, he slurred, "What happened, Munim? Nobody died at your house, did they?"

Shaking his head with a bit of annoyance, Munim matched Bilton's steps and said, "*Chhote Malik*, may God give you the strength to endure this. God has cast an evil eye on you. Oh God, have mercy."

Finally reaching his place and settling into his seat, Bilton mockingly slurred, "Hey, what's the riddle, Munim? What the hell has happened to me? Tell me."

"It's Damu—*Chhote Malik*," Munim stammered.

With droopy eyes, Bilton scoffed, letting out a derisive sound and in a single breath, Munim completed his sentence, "He has killed our master. He has murdered him." This time, true tears streamed down Munim's face.

As Bilton tried to pick up the half-empty glass of liquor he had set aside a long time ago, his hand slipped, sending the glass rolling to the other end of the table. His intoxicated bloodshot eyes, filled with a mix of shock and disbelief, froze on Munim's face. Looking at Bilton's slack-jawed expression, Munim recounted the entire incident. The stunned Badri and Bilton's two lackeys exchanged glances, alternating their gazes between Bilton and Munim.

When Munim finished, everyone seemed to catch a fleeting image of Ratnakar's imagined dead body. Everyone was silent. An announcement was made from the stage that there would be no more dancing tonight due to some special reason and that the bar would be closing. This happened once or twice a month. The bar owners would be tipped off in advance by the police's own people about the fake investigations. Later, they would come and indulge themselves, feasting and enjoying, while discreetly pocketing bribes, providing both blessings and support for future illegal activities. Needless to say, the two 'bouncers' of the bar were politely but firmly pushing the customers out after collecting their bills. This scene was often seen in the illegal bars of Mumbai and Delhi.

The first to break the silence was Jagga. "*Bhaiji*, inform the police—"

Clenching his teeth, Bilton stood up, his bloodshot eyes devoid of sorrow, filled instead with thoughts of revenge, and interrupted, "No, not the police. I will personally punish that son of a pig. Tonight will be his last night alive. Inform Lal Bhai, Rashid and Sankat. Tell them to surround that bastard's slum. That scoundrel must not escape. We will first go to the brick kiln. Leave the motorcycle at the school square. Let's go—Munim." In his intoxicated state, he slurred the last part of his speech. As he tried to leave, he stumbled and fell onto Badri. As Munim steadied him, Bilton glanced at Badri, restrained himself from saying anything, handed Jagga two five-hundred-rupee notes from the remaining gambling winnings, and said, "Settle the bill and follow us." Staggering, he left with Munim. Badri, initially not understanding, now grasped everything and felt a malicious glee, eagerly wishing for Damu's impending doom.

***

Without performing the night prayer, Jubed chained the door, dimmed the hurricane lamp, and set out with a torch. Pondering the ill omens, he entered Hariram's house through the back door in complete secrecy.

To Raimoni, her daughter's dishonour felt heavier than her husband's death. Stiff and silent, she sat at the corner of the bed near her husband's head, waiting for her son's return. At the foot of the bed, Sandhya sat with her head bowed, sharing the same depth of emotion. The upper portion of the lantern's chimney, placed on the floor, had turned completely black, making nothing clearly visible on Hariram's pain-stricken, lifeless face except for his bulging eyes. However, the tears on Sandhya's and Raimoni's faces, sitting on the floor, were vividly noticeable.

As Jubed entered the room and shone his torch on Hariram's lifeless body, he immediately realized that the disastrous hour of the night had struck this very room.

"Oh Allah! Have mercy. Sister, be patient. May Allah give you strength. Where is Damu?"

At the sound of Jubed's hushed voice, Raimoni and Sandhya, startled, looked at him and burst into tears. At the mention of Damu, a pang hit Sandhya's chest; she hadn't thought about him until now. Raimoni's grief-stricken mind grew suspicious seeing Jubed entering through the back door and speaking in a low voice. As she lifted her tear-streaked face with questioning eyes, Jubed said, "The owner has been murdered at the brick kiln. Damu went there. Munim has gone to inform Bilton. Where is Damu?"

Raimoni and Sandhya looked at each other in silence. Meanwhile, Damu, who had spent a long-time shedding tears beneath the banyan tree, had slowly gathered courage and strengthened his resolve, and had slowly made his way back home, entered through the back door. He had overheard Jubed's words.

At the sound of footsteps, everyone, including Raimoni, turned towards Damu. Raimoni stood up, pulling her son close, momentarily forgetting her husband's death, and exclaimed, "What have you done, my son?"

"I killed him. I punished him for his sins," Damu said these words with absolute calmness, looking directly at his mother. Seeing Jubed pull the sheet over Hariram's feet to cover his face, Damu cried out, "*Bapu*," and rushed to lay his head on

Hariram's chest, wailing. Raimoni placed her hand on his shoulder, startling him, and signalled for silence with her finger on her lips, saying, "Shh! Shh! Your father is gone. He wanted to see you stand on your own feet. He won't come back, but you can still return. Run, run away from here. Didn't you want to go to the city? Go—escape to some faraway place where no one will find you."

Sobbing through her tears, Sandhya tried to suppress her chest-wrenching cries, but Raimoni, weeping herself, spoke out to her, "Explain it to your brother, please. I've already lost my husband—don't want to lose my son too."

A sudden wave of sorrow hit Jubed, and tears unexpectedly rolled down his cheeks. He turned to Damu, trying to help Sandhya persuade him, saying, "Yes, son, run. If you live, your mother will survive."

With his face drenched in returning tears, Damu choked out, "So, should the only son flee, leaving his father's dead body behind? Should I abandon my helpless old mother to bear the burden of her husband's corpse and run away?"

The sharp-tongued Raimoni finally broke down. "Stop it, son. Don't say such things. You're all I have." Before she could finish her words, Damu stood up, wiped his tears, and regained his composure. "If we have to flee, we'll all go. But only after lighting my father's pyre." As soon as he said this in one breath and looked at Jubed, Jubed responded, "Then don't waste time. Let's go quickly. We need to chop the wood."

In silent agreement with her stubborn son's decision, Raimoni, forgetting everything in the urgency, quickly fetched an axe from inside and handed it to Damu. With tear-filled eyes, Damu headed towards the front door but then paused, turning to exit through the back door. Jubed followed behind, lighting the way with his torch.

***

Unlocking the door, Munim entered the office room and asked Bilton to steady himself. Still staggering, intoxicated, Bilton stumbled inside and said, "Turn on the light, Munim. I need to take one last look at my dead father's face before I leave."

Without using the torch, Munim pulled out a matchbox from his left pocket, lit the kerosene lamp that was kept in the corner under the bed. As he placed it on the bed, Bilton shuddered. Next to the broken TV lay Ratnakar's body. His tongue hung out from his terrified open mouth, and the blood around it had nearly dried. His eyes appeared as though they had burst out of their sockets. The torn *kurta* had ridden up from his waist over the dishevelled *dhoti*.

Even in the dim light of the lamp, Munim could see a tear at the corner of Bilton's bloodshot eyes, a sign of grief over his father's death.

"He beat up my father really bad – that bastard. But don't worry, Father. I'll make sure to settle the score, one by one." Though the words sounded almost comical, Bilton wiped his tears as he sat down heavily on the edge of the bed, head hanging low, his heart heavy with grief. Munim, having gone to Debu's room and not finding him there, returned and stood silently at the corner of the bed, a mute witness to the mourning.

After a long silence, the monotony was broken by the irritating, muffled sound of a ringtone coming from the pocket of Ratnakar's *kurta*. Bilton looked up, and as Munim approached, he froze in his tracks. Still dazed from intoxication, Bilton said, "Check it, Munim."

Munim didn't really want to touch the dead body, but now he had no choice. He hesitantly moved the body slightly and hurriedly pulled the mobile phone from the left pocket near the stomach, which had been ringing incessantly. With a questioning look, he glanced at the screen and said, "It's from home, *Chhote Malik.*"

"Give it to me."

Munim quickly pressed the button to receive the call and handed the phone to Bilton.

The only remaining member at home, unaware of everything that had transpired, spoke on the other end. Hearing his mother's voice, Bilton said, "Ma, I'm with Father. Father is going far away – so he won't come home tonight – and I'll be a little late too."

He explained the words with pauses, but the elderly woman, far from being satisfied, snapped back in her strong rural dialect, "Yes, yes, alright. He said he'd come home early today, that's why I called. And have you been drinking again? This morning you said you wouldn't touch the stuff anymore. Why do you drink this rubbish?..."

Bilton had run out of patience listening, and just at that moment, his two lackeys entered. He quickly cut the call, switched off the phone, and put it in his pocket, muttering in frustration,

"You've come. Listen – we need to wipe out that scoundrel's entire lineage. Burn down the whole slum. Just leave that bastard alive. I'll deal with him myself. Let's go."

Jagga, flashing the newly acquired, illegal, country-made revolver he'd gotten from Lal Singh, said as he started out, "Our other men have already gone to the slum."

With a grunt, Bilton snatched the revolver from Chhote Lal's hand, that he had collected from another fellow of Lal Singh, and began moving ahead. Munim, after a moment's thought, extinguished the lamp, left the door open, and turned on the torch. In the darkness, he saw Ratnakar's old jeep still parked in its usual spot and then followed the others. Before leaving, Munim took one last look at Ratnakar. Despite being a partner in most of his sins, it didn't once cross his mind that this gruesome death, though delivered by human hands, was nothing but the consequence of Ratnakar's countless transgressions.

****

Stumbling in a drunken stupor, Badri noticed the lights were still on inside as he wobbled through the outer gate. Frowning, he banged on the door, and Puja, with a heavy heart, had unlatched it from the inside. When the door didn't open immediately, Badri banged again. From inside, Puja called out, "The latch is locked from the outside, *baba*(father)."

It took a moment for Badri to process her words, but soon the memory of that afternoon came flooding back. Feeling even more uneasy, he remembered he himself had bolted it from the outside earlier. Unlocking the latch, he leaned against the doorframe, stumbled in, and asked, "You're not asleep yet?"

"A motherless girl with a drunk father doesn't find sleep easily," Puja replied with a quiet bitterness.

Puja's sarcastic remark went ignored by Badri, who, lost in his drunken haze, began savouring an imagined future of his own creation. He muttered, "Now we'll finally get some sleep. Once that wretched servant's son is dead, I also won't have to worry anymore."

Puja's suspicions were piqued by Badri's cryptic words, and she asked, "What are you talking about, *baba*?" In response, the drunken Badri, lowering his voice to keep it a secret, briefly revealed the murder of Ratnakar and Bilton's sinister plans. He then told her to lock the door and go to sleep and he himself staggered off to his room to sleep.

For several moments, Puja stood motionless, stunned. Gradually, a mixed feeling of fear and pain washed over her. As the memory of the day's horrific events of the sacrificial offering flashed in her mind, the fear dissolved into sorrowful tears welling up in her eyes. The weight of grief bore down on her heart as she silently stood there, tears streaming down her cheeks. After a few more moments of stillness, she walked out through the wide-open door and disappeared into the darkness.

***

Through the eerie darkness, with occasional flickers of Munim's torchlight falling from behind, Bilton, pausing intermittently, walked along the old cremation ground road, muttering repeatedly, " I will finish everyone off." About eight years ago, this place used to serve as the joint cremation ground for five villages. Since then, the cremation sites had been relocated, with three separate grounds established outside three different villages. Over time, the old large banyan tree, *peepal*, and *neem* trees here, along with the eucalyptus and other plants planted by the Panchayat under the forestry department, had grown, transforming the area into a small dense forest. Beyond this forest lay the *Dalit* slum.

***

Badri sat quietly for a while, lost in thought, about to lie down when his attention was caught by the flickering hurricane lamp light from the outer room. Thinking something was amiss, he went outside to check on his daughter, only to find that Puja was gone. The door was left wide open, just as he had left it when he entered.

"She has been blinded by love. This will certainly bring trouble," he muttered absentmindedly. Then, driven by paternal affection or sensing the impending danger his daughter might face, Badri left the house and started walking toward her likely destination in the darkness.

***

As Munim's torchlight swept through the dark, he suddenly spoke in a very low voice, "*Chhote Malik*, I think someone is heading that way!"

"Surround them. It's not one of us, is it?" Bilton stopped to consider the situation, his voice tinged with suspicion.

Keeping the torch switched off they approached the shadowy figure, encircling it in silence. When they finally shone the torchlight on the person, the figure's identity became clear—it was Puja, trying to shield her face with her hands.

The road in front of Puja's house, after a short distance to the right, had a narrow path to the left, just wide enough for one person to walk, which went straight through the forest and ended at the *dalit* settlement. This path, familiar from many dark nights, had been Puja's chosen route tonight. Meanwhile, coming from the direction of the brick kiln, Bilton and his men had approached from another path, which merged with this narrow path taken by Puja at the last stretch of the forest, almost before reaching the settlement.

In fear, anxiety, and sorrow, Pooja had caught a brief glimpse of the torchlight, but it didn't register in her mind at all.

Now, hearing the voice from behind the blinding light, she realized it was the arrival of the devil himself, and her limbs went numb. Ignoring everything else, Bilton's habitual mockery emerged from his lips, "Wow! Come to meet your future husband in the middle of the night? Did your father, I mean my 'dear father-in-law,' send you?"

Puja stood silent, clenching her teeth, as if trying to channel her fire of anger to summon strength.

"So, what's wrong? —has your mouth been stitched shut? This morning, you were running your mouth like firecrackers," Bilton taunted. Though his words were both disjointed and sarcastic, his tone clearly carried his anger and thirst for revenge.

"What did you say then? 'vile deeds', 'gambler'— yes, now I'll show you real 'vile deeds'—a wedding night before the marriage!" Bilton advanced one step at a time while Puja retreated one step, equally matched in pace. Suddenly, her foot hit something on the ground, and she realized it was a tree branch. Instantly, considering it as her only means of self-defence, she grabbed the branch and began swinging it wildly, shouting, "Forget your wedding dreams, scoundrel! Get out of my way!"

Bilton was about to pull out his revolver and threaten her, but one of the strikes from the branch knocked it out of his hand. Puja made several frantic futile attempts consecutively to hit him with the branch, and then while one of her blows landed successfully, Bilton quickly grabbed hold of the branch, yanking it with force behind him. The sudden jerk caused the branch to fly out of Puja's hands, and she stumbled, losing balance and finding herself nearly within Bilton's breath. And before she could step back, Bilton grabbed her arm below the shoulder with a tight grip.

"What did you think? I don't know—you're going to warn that swine?" Bilton hissed with menace as Puja, struggling unsuccessfully to free herself, retorted fiercely, "Yes, I am going there. Let go of me, you scoundrel! Ugh!"

Intoxicated and with brute strength, Bilton tried to pin Puja to the ground, gritting his teeth and lustfully growling, "Now I'll show you, you bitch—this 'vile deed'—I'll do it right in front of everyone."

Underneath him, Puja fought back, pushing him away with both hands and attempting to kick him off. Just as she was about to break free,

Bilton grabbed the zipper of her *kurta*, ripping it apart as the back tore. In her desperate attempt to cover herself, Puja failed to escape, leaving her bare back exposed to Bilton's touch. Though hidden by the darkness, the faces of the three men standing around reflected a mix of satisfaction, curiosity, and lust. Helpless, Puja pressed with all her might, using her hands and heels, and cried out in anguish, "You sinner, know this—your father was killed by Damu, and you will meet the same fate!"

"Don't worry," Bilton growled through gritted teeth, "we'll have our wedding night first, and then I'll send your lover to the afterlife." As he spoke, he ripped the rest of Puja's *kameez* completely, freeing her hands. Seizing the moment, Puja slapped him across the face and spat in his direction, her voice trembling as she tearfully pleaded, "Let me go, you bastard!"

Bilton, filled with rage, grabbed both of her hands and shouted, "I'll let you go, alright. Hey, hold this bitch's arms down!"

To enforce his command, Jagga and Chhote Lal stepped forward. Standing on either side of Puja they pressed their feet down onto her wrists, pinning her hands to the ground. In a state of despair, physical pain, and sorrow, Puja began sobbing helplessly.

Fuelled by both anger and lust, Bilton swiftly straddled her thighs and yanked her torn kurta aside, exposing her further as he continued his vile assault.

In the pitch-black night, amidst the dark forest, the lustful eyes of the four human-like monsters, driven by their vile desires, could see a twisted vision—Puja's fully exposed upper body shining brightly in their mixed reality of lust and delusion.

In a very short span of time, as Puja's terrified and pleading cries filled the air, Bilton forcefully entered her. The clear stars and planets in the open sky, witnessing the horrific scene through the gaps in the trees, seemed to draw a veil of clouds to hide their faces in shame.

***

Badri was certain that Puja would take the path leading to the slum. Despite his unsteady head, he moved forward as cautiously as possible. The sound of Puja's crying now reached his ears and he froze in place, trying to pinpoint the direction of the sound. Though his voice refused to emerge from his throat, with an emotion-laden, trembling tone, he repeatedly called her name as he quickened his pace toward the source of her cries.

As he moved forward a little and tried to see more clearly, he thought he saw several shadowy figures standing not too far ahead. One more figure had just stood up from the ground, while someone else seemed to be lying at his feet.

In reality, Bilton had stood up, buckling his belt, and had picked up the revolver that had fallen from his hand a short while ago.

Writhing in unbearable pain, Puja cursed in a strangled voice, "You will die! God will punish you!"

Without paying any attention to her words, Bilton spoke, "Hey, you all have a taste of her youth too. Leave her in such a state that she can't face anyone in the morning."

By this time, everything had become clear to Badri. Calling out his daughter's name, he rushed forward to save her, but Bilton blocked his way. From beneath Jagga, Puja's heart-wrenching cries broke out, "Save me, *baba*!"

Drunken Badri now tried to summon the strength of a father, Badri Prasad, as he cried out, "Hey, Bilton, let go of my daughter."

"I will—of course, I will let her go. After everyone's done with her. And after that, you can make her work the streets. We'll be your permanent customers," Bilton declared without a shred of hesitation, as if dropping the final curtain on the grim drama he had authored that morning.

Struggling against him, Badri grabbed Bilton by the throat, displaying the righteous wrath of a Brahmin, "I'll kill you! You beast in human form!"

Seeing things take a turn for the worse, Bilton, with all his strength, broke free and shoved Badri violently. Badri was thrown several feet away, crashing hard onto the ground. His head struck directly on an old, jagged brick or stone lying there. A small, pained groan escaped from his lips due to the sudden intense pain. At that very moment, from Puja's trembling lips came the faintest utterance—just one word, "*baba.*"

Blood was slowly soaking the ground beneath Badri's head. For the last time, he gazed at Pooja, his trembling lips attempting to form words, but he couldn't speak. His half-open eyes, filled with tears of sorrow, disgust, and regret, reflected the agony he felt. Just before everything around him went still, it seemed to him as though another monstrous beast was tearing his beloved daughter's bloodied heart from her chest and gnawing on it viciously.

***

Damu had already gathered quite a bit of wood, some large dry logs and some smaller green branches. Jubed was piling the wood in one spot. Looking at Jubed with a weary, sweat-drenched face, Damu said, "*Chacha*, we won't be able to reach the cremation ground. We'll have to set up the pyre somewhere here."

"Yes, then the empty spot next to the old cremation ground should be fine. I'll take some wood and leave it there, and you check for more dry wood in the other direction." Jubed spoke in a low voice as he hoisted a few logs onto his shoulder and started walking, while Damu, axe in hand, ventured deeper into the jungle in search of more dry wood.

***

Bilton and his gang had reached the empty space between the *dalit* slum and the edge of the jungle. From here, both the slum and the jungle were clearly visible.

"Where are they all?" Bilton, seeing no one around, asked in a tone of frustration.

Jagga, casting a worried glance while signalling with the dimming light of his torch, replied, "I told Lal *bhai* and Sankat to come here. Rashid was supposed to encircle the slum."

Needless to say, that during Puja's gang rape, Jagga had taken the torch from Munim.

Since mobile phones weren't common yet, only Lal Singh had one, and even that had already been declared switched off.

"All of them are useless scum," Bilton cursed in anger, leaving everyone with no choice but to wait.

***

Damu, lost in thought, had ventured quite a bit inward. Suddenly, it seemed to him that someone might be lying a few steps behind. When he went back to check, Damu's heart sank. His eyes filled with tears again.

Puja, completely naked except for the salwar slipped down below her knees, was lying curled up with her head drooped onto her left shoulder.

Her left hand was stretched out on the ground, and her right hand, half-clenched in the dirt, silently conveyed her unsuccessful attempt to rise.

In a choked voice, Damu called out Puja's name. Though her name reached her fractured mind, her slightly open, tear-soaked eyes couldn't form an image of Damu's reflection. When he tried to shake her awake, Puja, imagining yet another monster attacking her, whimpered in a trembling voice, "Let me go – let me go – let me go."

Overwhelmed with grief, Damu cried out, "It's me, Puja – see, it's your Damu."

In a renewed effort, regaining some awareness, Puja looked at him, took his hand in hers, and with tear-filled eyes, glanced around before uttering "*baba*" pointing toward something with her hand as she began to sob.

Following her gesture, Damu saw Badri's still figure. He quickly covered Puja with the torn *kameez* lying beside her and stepped toward Badri. As Puja tried to move and failed, whimpering in pain, Damu hurried back. He lifted Puja into his arms, picked up the axe, and rushed toward Badri.

Setting Puja down beside her father's lifeless body, he gently touched Badri's shoulder and called out, "Uncle." As he nudged him slightly, Badri's head rolled off the sharp stone it had been resting on and onto the ground. Puja, heartbroken at the loss of her father, burst into tears, wailing, "That devil has killed my father."

"Who? Him?" Damu asked, almost confirming what he already knew.

Puja nodded her head weakly, speaking in halting, pain-laced words, "They've come to kill you. Go check on *kaki*(aunty) and *didi*. That devil is capable of anything."

Damu carefully covered Puja's body with the *kameez*, lifted her along with the axe, and started walking toward the *dalit* slum, saying, "I'll take revenge. Today itself. I swear by God."

"Leave me here by my *baba*."

"No, I'll take you to Ma first. Then I'll kill each one of them," Damu replied, quickening his pace.

"But after all this, I no longer want to live, Damu." Overwhelmed with pain and despair, Puja became distraught.

"Don't say that. It will weaken me." With intense fury, Damu's legs moved swiftly through the darkness, gaining speed.

***

One by one, Lal, Sankat, and Rashid Ali joined Bilton. Two young men who had come with Rashid stood guard on either side of the slum, armed with *kukris*. Rashid conveyed the news he received from one of the guards to Bilton: "*Bhai Ji*, that bastard may have escaped. Sampat entered through the back of his house. His father is likely dead, and his mother and sister are sitting silently by the bed."

"The slum rats must've helped the swine escape. But if he knows about his father's death, he'll still be hiding nearby. Lock every door, burn the whole slum down. If anyone tries to escape, shoot them or hack them to pieces—don't let even a single one survive. *That is right.* Go now, hurry up —wreak havoc!"

With this authoritative order that sounded like a fiery speech, Sankat and Rashid wasted no time and immediately dashed toward the slum, just a few feet away. Noticing Lal still standing there, Bilton's suspicion flared, and he shot a direct question at him: "What's wrong with you? Are you a damn 'traitor'?"

Though it couldn't be seen in the darkness, fury seemed to blaze from Lal Singh's eyes. "*Bhai ji*, if anyone else had said that, I would've either strangled him or shot him and sent him to the afterlife. But, *bhai ji*, I owe you a debt of loyalty. I'm part of your group — otherwise, just like I supply weapons, I also know how to use them. I had no hand in Damu's escape. Anyway, let's leave that aside, *bhai ji*. My sister lives in the slum, and she's pregnant. Politics may have targeted this slum many times, but it's always stayed quiet. Today, I'm asking you — leave this slum alone, *bhai ji*."

"And what if I don't? Will you strangle me? Shoot me? Go ahead, shoot – shoot me," replied Bilton mockingly.

In the middle of Bilton's words, just as Lal Singh reached into his pocket to pull out his pistol, Bilton, understanding his intent, swiftly kicked him hard and, in an instant, fired a bullet into Lal Singh's head. "A crow in peacock's feathers, you bastard," Bilton spat.

Moments later, the entire *dalit* settlement was

engulfed in a terrifying, blazing inferno.

It goes without saying at this point that Sankat and his group were affiliated with a non-political organization that supported a particular political party in this province. This organization, notorious or famed throughout the region under the name of a certain "*Sena*," (army) had gained infamy over the years. In recent years, they had been involved in numerous brutal incidents, especially targeting *Dalits* and other so-called lower-caste groups with merciless killings. The reason behind these atrocities stemmed from the twisted beliefs of their patrons, who operated under the notion that these oppressed and persecuted *Dalits* were directly or indirectly supporting an opposing faction.

***

With wood on his shoulders, Jubed had just emerged from the jungle near the old cremation ground when the faint commotion he'd heard moments earlier became a clear, heart-wrenching cry of anguish. He stood frozen in disbelief as he saw the slum engulfed in a ferocious fire. And just then, a bullet struck the load of wood on his head.

It was Jagga who had fired at him after spotting Jubed in the light of the blazing inferno consuming the slum. Missing his first shot, Jagga fired again as he and Chhote Lal rushed toward Jubed. In panic, Jubed dropped all the wood and ran, shouting in desperation toward Damu to warn him. "Damu, run! Run! The devils—" His warning never finished. In the dim half-light, the terrified old man's steps couldn't match the powerful strides of the pursuing demons, and the third bullet struck him in the left side of his back. A few birds startled from nearby trees and flew off to settle elsewhere.

"Have mercy—*Ya Allah. La Ilaha Illallah Muhammadur Rasulullah...*" Uttering the name of his beloved deity, the devout, benevolent, and pious Muslim, Jubed Ali Khan, breathed his last.

***

Jubed's scream and the sound of gunfire both reached Damu's ears. In fact, he had seen Jubed fall to the ground after being shot. Not fully understanding the situation, Damu gently placed Puja behind a large tree, whispering for her to stay quiet, and ran with his axe to Jubed. Calling out '*chacha*' and shaking him, he found Jubed already lifeless. Before his tear-filled eyes could blur everything, another gunshot rang out. The bullet hit the tree right next to Damu. Jumping from one tree to another to avoid the last two bullets, Damu hurled his axe at Jagga with full force. With deadly precision, the sharp edge of the axe hit Jagga squarely on the shoulder.

"None of you will survive now," Damu shouted, rushing forward to pick up the axe and swiftly bringing it down on Jagga's head. Jagga, bleeding profusely, writhed on the ground in agony. His constant companion, Chhote Lal, a master at throwing knives, hurled his knife at Damu, but Damu's sudden crouch made it miss by a hair's breadth.

Meanwhile, Puja, in a failed attempt to stand, collapsed, clutching her lower abdomen in pain, and wailed, "*Baba*, I'm coming to you!"

Turning swiftly, Damu ran toward Chhote Lal and landed a forceful kick to his stomach. Before Chhote Lal could even think of retaliating or getting back on his feet, Damu swung the axe down on his chest. With a brief groan, Chhote Lal—aka Chhutku—lay still, lifeless.

***

The slum was blazing fiercely.

The almost half-dead, newly widowed Raimoni, in a futile attempt to save her husband's corpse with her daughter's help, perished in the flames along with her daughter. A few who had managed to escape the clutches of the all-consuming flames ultimately succumbed to bullets and *kukri* strikes. Yet, even in their dying breaths, they latched onto the two kukri-wielding youths with a death grip, dragging them down in a final, fatal embrace. With their last ounce of strength, they hurled themselves back into the inferno, taking their killers with them into the blazing abyss.

Rashid Ali, driven by a twisted desire, shot the husband of Lal Singh's young, pregnant sister and sought to force himself upon her. However, her fierce spirit ignited a desperate struggle. In a moment of defiance, she delivered a powerful kick to his groin, causing him to stagger. Seizing her chance, she wrested his gun away and shot him, the bullet striking true. As he lay dying, Rashid, with the last remnants of his strength, pulled her close, their bodies entwined in a final embrace. Together, they succumbed to the roaring flames of the inferno, finding their eternal rest in the embrace of fire.

Lal Singh's wife and the other family members, gripped by the fear of gunfire and overcome with political chaos, stood silently on the roof, shedding tears as helpless spectators. Meanwhile, on the far side of the field, the villagers regarded the burning slum as if it were a *Diwali* night, adorned with a garish display of lights. They engaged in animated discussions, exchanging thoughts on the swift flames and the details of the unfolding chaos, speculating about the various reasons behind the event and the possible consequences that would follow.

***

After Sankat returned and relayed all the news to Bilton, he showed no sorrow for the deaths of the hired goons. Instead, he reveled in the success of wiping out Damu's family along with the entire *dalit* slum. His voice, still slightly slurred from enough intoxication, gave the command, "Don't worry. You'll get all the money now. Tomorrow, I'll fabricate a case at the police station. I want that bastard. Jagga and Chhutku are already after him. You go too. Bring him in, or kill him if you have to. Half my revenge is already complete. *'That is right'*. You go with Munim. I'm coming too."

Even before he finished speaking, Sankat had already started walking toward the jungle. Munim followed closely behind. Bilton, keeping a slight distance, trailed after them.

***

Carrying the bloodied axe, Damu, after ensuring the deaths of the two demons who had killed his father-figure 'Jubed *chacha*', returned to Puja, splattered with blood on his hands, clothes, and face.

"I've sent two of them to hell. Two more to go," he said, his voice gritty with resolve.

By now, Puja had understood everything. In response to his words of reassurance, she broke down in tears and cried out, "If you've become a killer, then kill them all! Leave no one alive. Look! Those devils have set the entire slum on fire."

In the span of just a few hours, Damu felt as though he had lost nearly everything in his life. But now, as he listened to Puja's words and looked toward the slum engulfed in the silent inferno, with flames roaring like an uncontrollable wildfire on the jungle's edge, he realized that in this very moment, he truly had lost everything— his father, mother, sister—everything.

Just as he was about to cry out "Ma!" and rush toward the fire, a gunshot rang out, and a bullet struck his left shoulder, knocking him backward. Despite the force of the shot, the physical pain barely registered in the face of his overwhelming grief over losing his mother and the burning desire for vengeance. The intense sorrow and rage numbed him to the wound.

Grabbing the axe he'd forgotten, he charged towards Sankat, who was now emerging like a shadowy figure from the jungle. Sankat tried to fire again, but his gun clicked empty. He frantically searched his pockets for more bullets, but before he could decide whether to advance or retreat, Damu leaped forward with lightning speed and brought the axe down on his neck.

The brutal slaying left Damu looking like a bloodthirsty tiger. After the savage act, he instinctively sought cover behind a tree, his senses now sharp, ready for whatever came next.

The dim beam of Munim's dying flashlight, barely stronger than the flickering light from the burning slum, cut through the darkness as he approached cautiously. When his foot brushed against Jagga's lifeless body, he shrieked in horror. In that very instant, Damu sprang from behind a tree and swung his axe. But his grip had loosened with exhaustion, and instead of the sharp edge, the blunt iron end of the axe struck Munim square in the face. He was sent sprawling, nearly flipping backward, as blood gushed from his mouth, a few broken teeth spilling onto the ground. Before Damu could lift his axe for another strike, a gunshot rang out from behind, and a bullet pierced his right shoulder, sending him crashing to the ground, axe still in his hand.

Ignoring the searing pain, Damu gritted his teeth and, in a desperate lunge, crawled toward Munim, who was groaning in agony. He drove the axe into Munim's chest, then dropped it to clasp his hands around Munim's throat, strangling him with sheer rage. "I'll send every sinner to the underworld with my own hands today," he hissed through clenched teeth, as he yanked Munim off the ground. But just as he was about to finish the job, a second gunshot rang out. The bullet tore through Munim's back. Already dead, Munim seemed to die once more, as if by a twisted act of atonement for his countless sins, taking his master's bullet and unwittingly saving Damu in the process. And now, Damu, weakened and wounded, watched as Bilton slowly approached, his figure looming clearly before him in the dim light.

"Today, you'll die by my hands, you son of a swine," Bilton snarled, drawing out each word as he prepared to fire his third shot. But before he could pull the trigger, Damu, in a flash, hurled the axe with all his might. This time, the blunt end of the axe struck Bilton's leg hard, causing him to drop the gun a few feet away. Without giving him the chance to pick it up, Damu charged at him like a raging bull, ramming him with his head. Then, with a swift kick, he growled, "Tomorrow, the whole world will see what happens to those who oppress the poor when they finally rise up."

As Bilton lay on the ground listening to the words of Damu, his hand brushed against Chhote Lal's knife. Just as Damu swung his second kick, Bilton thrust the knife straight into Damu's stomach. The force of the kick, landing squarely on Bilton's midsection, caused him to groan in pain and release the knife's handle. Enduring the searing agony, Damu quickly yanked the blade from his own gut, and in one swift motion, plunged it into Bilton's abdomen, twisting it with vengeful fury. The vision of his mother and sister's burning bodies flashed before his eyes, fuelling his rage. The more Damu twisted the knife, the louder Bilton's screams of agony grew. Moments later, as Bilton's body weakened, Damu withdrew the blade and drove it straight into his chest. With Bilton writhing in pain, Damu knelt on his chest, his hands tightening around his throat. After ensuring the final enemy had breathed his last, Damu rose, his eyes falling upon the smoldering, dying flames engulfing the slum. A gut-wrenching cry escaped him as the full weight of his loss hit him. At that moment, unbearable pain coursed through his entire body. Staggering, he began calling out Puja's name, each step more faltering than the last.

Puja, having already tried once unsuccessfully to stand, was dragging her pain-ridden body toward Damu. As Damu moved towards her, something brushed against his foot. He glanced down and nudged it with his foot, then bent down to pick it up. But, unable to hold his balance, he collapsed to the ground. Groaning in pain, he felt around in the dirt and lifted what had touched his foot—it was Bilton's gun. He cocked the gun, paused for a moment in thought, his face full of sorrow, and then began dragging himself forward once again.

Hearing Damu's voice, Puja called out to him in a voice strained with pain. Both of them crawled across the ground until they came within an arm's reach of each other under a tree. Damu, hiding the gun, painfully propped himself up against the tree and pulled Puja to sit beside him. As she struggled to sit up, Puja, trying to dispel her deep-seated fears, asked softly, "Are you alright?"

With his bloodied body struggling to gather its fading strength, Damu ignored Puja's question and said, "I've killed them all. No one's left alive. Those demons were so cruel, I couldn't even light my father's funeral pyre. He burned in the very fire they set. Mother became a *'sati'* in that fire—my sister was consumed by it too. I couldn't do anything. There's no point in me staying alive anymore."

Through her tear-choked voice, Puja protested desperately, "No, no, don't say that. You have to live. I'm the one who should die. I can't bear the weight of this shame. Free me from this unbearable life. Strangle me. If I die by your hands, I'll find peace. Otherwise, I'll have to take my own life."

Damu, having already made up his mind, responded with a grim contradiction, "And who should I live for? To end up on the gallows?"

"Then let's both die together. Why don't you

answer me?" Puja asked her last question, her voice breaking as she stared at the silent Damu, her cheeks drenched in tears.

"That's how it will be. We'll both die together," Damu said, as a dry, painful smile briefly touched his lips, tears flowing steadily down his face. He gently pulled Puja to his chest on the left side, and with his right hand, he drew the gun. As Puja, spiritually prepared for her final release, leaned into him, he kissed her forehead, tears streaming down, and pulled the trigger.

A few birds flew off from the sheltering tree above.

Then, laying Puja's lifeless body gently on his lap, Damu placed the gun beneath his own ear and pulled the trigger once more – for the last time.

The remaining birds from the nearby trees fluttered their wings and soared into the sky, vanishing somewhere in the direction of the waning crescent moon of the eighth night of the dark fortnight.

***

Epilogue

The next morning, as the sun rose higher, whispers of the news reached the ears of the police, prompting them to arrive and investigate. Under political pressure, the brutal incident was declared to be the result of a personal vendetta. All political parties condemned the act vehemently, and the misrepresented account of the incident made the front page of the local newspaper the following day. Three days later, the story was relegated to a tiny news piece in the corner of several major newspapers.

That night, Debu, also known as Debnayaran, made his way straight to the station, where he stealthily boarded a slowly departing train from the platform without a ticket, only to discover that it was bound for Howrah.

After that, no one ever heard anything further about him.

Between 1997 and 2000, numerous brutal murders led to the conviction of their perpetrators in the district court, resulting in death sentences in 2010. However, in 2013, the state high court acquitted them due to a lack of sufficient evidence. Such incidents continue to occur across India every day.

How will justice be served and when?

THE END

9 798339 956075